With the help of beautiful, full-colour illustrations, diagrams and simple clear text, this first Picture Encyclopedia will encourage learning and stimulate young minds.
This encyclopedia contains an exciting variety of subjects and fascinating facts.
A long-lasting book of interest and information to read and enjoy.

Written by Anne McKie. Illustrated by Ken McKie.
Text and illustration © 1993 Grandreams Limited.

This edition published in 1995.

Published by
GRANDREAMS LIMITED
Jadwin House, 205/211 Kentish Town Road, London, NW5 2JU.

Printed in Czech Republic.

GK1

# THE FUN-TO-LEARN
# PICTURE ENCYCLOPEDIA

# Contents

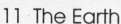

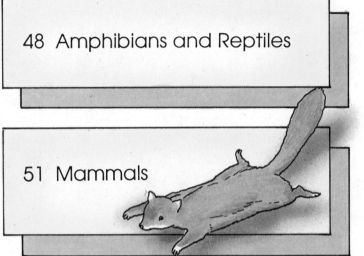

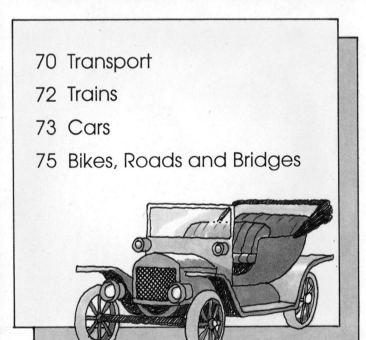
7

Venus

Sun

Mars

Earth

Jupiter

Mercury

Saturn

The Earth orbits the Sun, and the Moon orbits the Earth.

## The Solar System

Our solar system is made up of nine planets that travel in orbit around the Sun. They are Mercury, Venus, Earth, Mars, Jupiter, Saturn, Uranus, Neptune and Pluto, together with a ring of asteroids. These are thousands of pieces of rock between Mars and Jupiter.

The Sun is the biggest thing we can see when we look into the sky. It is a huge star that gives out heat and light. The planets produce no light of their own and, like the Earth, get their warmth and light from the Sun.

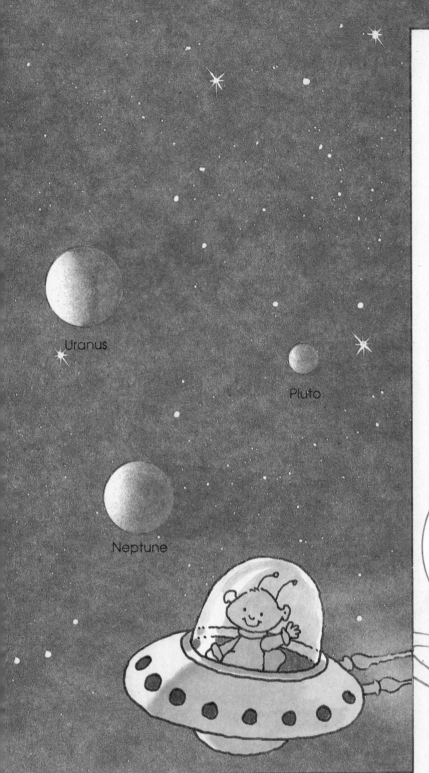

## The Planets

There are nine planets that circle the Sun. Together they are called the solar system. Our Earth is one of the smaller planets.

**Mercury**
58 million km (36 million miles) from the Sun, no moon, orbits the Sun every 88 days.

**Venus**
108 million km (67 million miles) from the Sun, no moon, orbits the Sun every 225 days.

**Earth**
150 million km (93 million miles) from the Sun, one moon, orbits the Sun every 365¼ days.

**Mars**
228 million km (142 million miles) from the Sun, two moons, orbits the Sun every 687 days.

**Jupiter**
778 million km (480 million miles) from the Sun, 16 moons, orbits the Sun every 11.86 years.

**Saturn**
1,427 million km (886 million miles) from the Sun, 17 moons, orbits the Sun every 29.46 years.

**Uranus**
2,870 million km (1,783 million miles) from the Sun, 15 moons, orbits the Sun every 84 years.

**Neptune**
4,500 million km (2,800 million miles) from the Sun, three moons, orbits the Sun every 165 years.

**Pluto**
5,970 million km (3,700 million miles) from the Sun, one moon, orbits the Sun every 248 years.

## The Sun

The Sun's diameter is 100 times bigger than the Earth's. It is really just a ball of super hot gas. The temperature at the centre of the Sun is 15,000,000°C and 5,500°C on the surface.

The Earth is 149,637,000km (93,000,000 miles) from the Sun. If we were any nearer, it would be too hot and all life would die out.

You must never look directly at the Sun with a telescope or binoculars as the brightness would damage your eyes.

2800°C

800°C

100°C

# The Moon

The Moon is the Earth's satellite. It revolves around the Earth once every 29.5 days, at a distance of about 250,000 km.

The Moon has no light of its own. What we call moonlight is just reflected sunlight.

We always see the same side of the Moon, astronauts have taken pictures of the dark side from their spacecrafts.

On the surface of the Moon are great craters and mountain ranges, but no water, air or vegetation. And there is no sign of life, past or present.

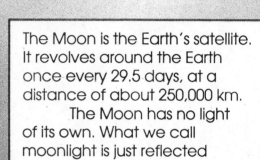

**Why does the Moon seem to change shape?** As the Moon goes around the Earth, the Sun lights up different parts of it. To us on Earth, the Moon seems to change shape every night. These shapes are called phases and repeat every 29 days.

The Earth acts like a magnet pulling everything to itself. This is why objects fall to the ground and why we feel heavy. On the Moon gravity is much weaker so we would feel lighter.

In July 1969 America sent a manned spacecraft to the Moon. The first man to walk on the Moon's dry, dusty surface was Neil Armstrong from the crew of the Apollo II.

# The Earth

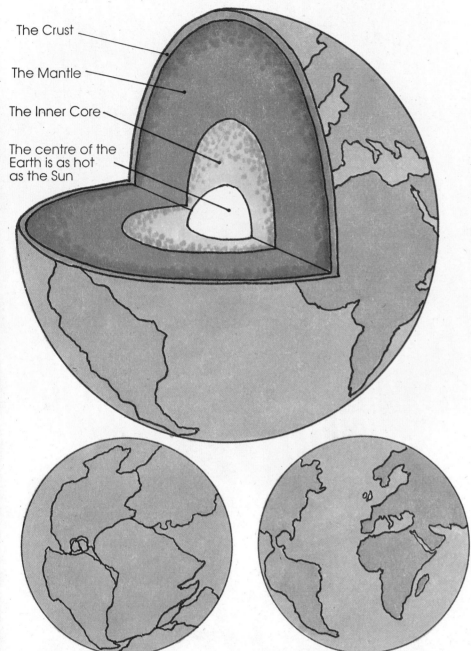

- The Crust
- The Mantle
- The Inner Core
- The centre of the Earth is as hot as the Sun

Earth is the planet on which we all live. Scientists believe that about 5,000 million years ago, a swirling mass of boiling hot rocks and gases, revolving around the Sun, changed into a ball of liquid rock that formed the Earth.

Very slowly, over hundreds of millions of years, the Earth cooled down and a hard crust formed on the outside.

Sometimes the hot gases and liquid broke through the crust, moving and cracking the surface. This formed mountains and cut deep trenches that later formed the ocean beds.

Millions of years went by, the Earth became cooler and great clouds of vapour covered the Earth and fell as rain. This made the rivers and lakes and filled up the seas and oceans.

Did you know that three-quarters of our planet is covered by water?

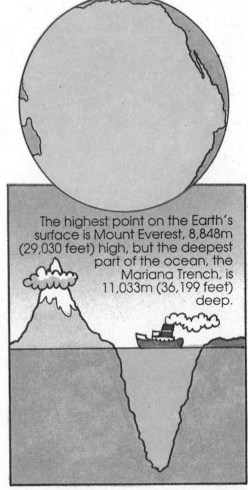

The highest point on the Earth's surface is Mount Everest, 8,848m (29,030 feet) high, but the deepest part of the ocean, the Mariana Trench, is 11,033m (36,199 feet) deep.

Scientists believe that all the continents were once joined together in one great mass called Pangaea. This broke up and formed the continents that we know today.

**Weight and Dimension**
If your bathroom scales were big enough you would find that the Earth weighed about 6,000 million, million, million tonnes!

The Earth's 'waist' measurement, round the equator, is over 40,000 km (24,856 miles).

11

Our Earth is always slowly changing. The sea, the rain, the wind and the frost break down the rocks and wear away the surface. This happens very slowly. It is called erosion.

# Volcanoes

Some changes happen suddenly! Although the Earth feels cool on the surface, it is very hot inside.

Sometimes the red hot lava and gases find a weak spot in the Earth's crust and suddenly burst through. Ash, red-hot cinders and boiling lava spread over the land, often covering whole towns.

Some volcanoes erupt under the sea. After a while, when the red-hot lava cools, a new island may be formed.

## Earthquakes

Earthquakes often happen in those parts of the world where volcanoes occur.

The rock deep beneath the Earth's surface moves, then splits and cracks appear along a weak point in the Earth's crust.

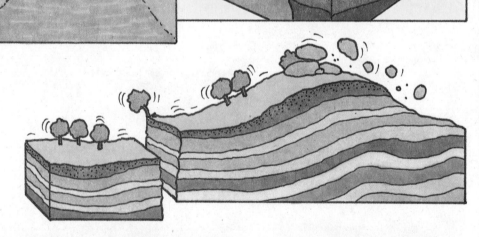

A big earthquake can cause enormous waves in the sea. These huge tidal waves can cause terrible floods, often many miles inland.

# Rivers

Rivers begin in mountains or hills as small trickles of rainwater or melting snow. Trickles flow together to form streams and these join other streams to form a river. The river becomes slower and broader as it winds across the land and reaches the sea at the river's mouth.

When a river comes to the edge of a cliff, it plunges down forming a waterfall.

A glacier is a slow moving river of ice. It creeps down the valley taking large rocks with it. It melts as it reaches the warmer, lower lands.

### The Grand Canyon
This has been cut out of the solid rock by the Colorado River over millions of years. It is up to 1.6 km (1 mile) deep.

# The Earth's Climate

The words 'weather' and 'climate' have quite different meanings.

When someone tells you that it has been warm and sunny that day, they are talking about the weather.

If they say that the Sahara Desert is always hot and the Arctic is always cold, they are talking about the climate of these places, which has been the same for a very long time.

Temperature, rainfall, winds and ocean currents all affect the climate. And how far north or south of the equator a place is, determines whether it is hot or cold.

The temperature falls as you go up a mountain. There are mountains on the equator, the hottest part of the Earth, with snow on their peaks all the year round.

In some large countries the land in the middle is often hot and dry. The moist winds from the sea never reach inland, so there is very little rainfall.

"Hello, I live in the tropical rainforest, you can see me on page 16."

As the Earth spins around the Sun it tilts on its axis. Near the equator the Sun is almost overhead, so it is always hot and the rays are very strong.

As they spread out towards the poles over a wider area, the Sun's rays are weaker and the land is cooler.

North Pole

Equator

Cold Zone North

Cool Zone

Warm Zone

Hot Zone

Warm Zone

Cold Zone South

South Pole

15

# The Tropical Rainforest

"It's me again, I'm a Toucan and this is my home."

A tropical rainforest is a hot and steamy place, rather like an enormous greenhouse! It has a temperature of around 26°C (79°F) most of the time, and 150cm (60in) of rain falls each year.

The trees and plants in this densely packed forest grow very quickly in the hot, humid climate, where very little sunlight ever reaches the forest floor.

Vegetation grows so close and tangled that it forms a thick green curtain as it reaches up towards the sunlight.

Because the temperature hardly ever changes, the flowers and plants are some of the biggest in the world. The trees are amongst the tallest, forming a giant canopy on top of the rainforest.

# Who lives in a rainforest?

At different levels the rainforest provides a home for thousands of plants and creatures:

**Emergent layer**
This layer consists of the tops of the tallest trees, often over 40m (130ft).

**Canopy layer**
This is where most of the animals are found as there is plenty of food and the trees form a sturdy platform.
        Many of the animals and birds are very rare and cannot be found anywhere else in the world.

**Middle layer**
The trees are not so densely packed. Flowers and ferns grow in this shady layer.
        Of the 8,600 types of bird that we know, more than half can be found in the rainforests.

**Shrub layer**
Light is scarce in this layer and the trees reach only 5m (16ft). Over a million species of insect live here and most of them have never been seen before.

**Herb layer**
Only herbs and seedlings grow on the dark forest floor. New growth is rare.

**The Harpy Eagle**
This large bird searches in the tall trees for food - monkeys!

**Bats**
Many different bats like the 'Flying Fox' live here.

**The Howler Monkey**
Its loud call can be heard 1.6km (1 mile) away.

**Sloth**
This slow moving animal spends all its time hanging upside down.

**Iguana**
This is just one of the many lizards that live in the rainforest.

**Jaguar**
The only big cat in the S. American rainforest, it will eat most animals and can catch fish.

**Marsupial Frog**
Young frogs develop in their mother's pouch.

**Tree Boa**
A large snake that kills by squeezing its victim.

**Coati**
These little scavengers roam the forest in large bands.

**Tapir**
As big as a small cow, this shy animal feeds on leaves and vegetation.

**Bushmaster**
Silent, deadly killer of the forest floor.

Millions of beautiful butterflies live in the rainforests.

And many many more...

17

# Where do you find the rainforests?

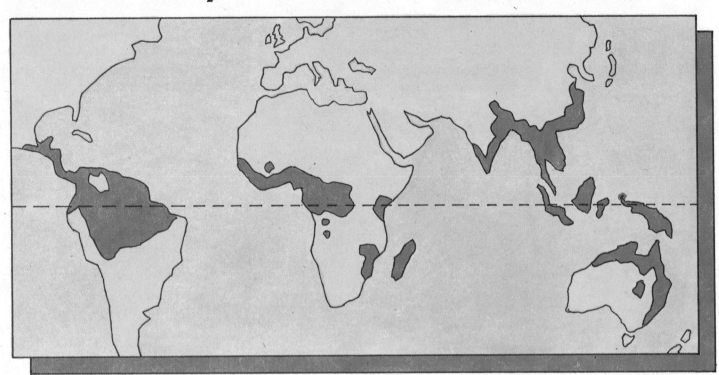

They stretch around the Equator, with at least half of them in Central and South America. There the world's biggest rainforest covers over 6.5 million sq. km (2.5 million sq. miles). The River Amazon flows through this forest for more than half its length, over 3,220 km (2,000 miles). Often the only way to travel through the dense forest is by river.

More rainforest can be found in West Africa, Madagascar, Sri Lanka, Burma, Malaysia, Indonesia, New Guinea and Australia.

## Why do we need rainforests?

Trees and plants have a very important part to play in keeping the Earth's air supply pure. If we destroyed all the forests, there would be no trees left to take the carbon dioxide and give out the oxygen that we need to breathe. This would cut off the world's air supply.

Many people think of the rainforest as the Earth's lungs!

We breathe in oxygen and breathe out carbon dioxide. Plants use this carbon dioxide to make more oxygen.

Most of us will never be able to visit a rainforest, but some of the flowers and plants can be seen in the big heated glasshouses at botanical gardens.

# What is happening to the rainforests?

In the last few years, great areas of forest have been destroyed as people have moved in. We have cut down the trees for timber, dug great holes in the Earth to find minerals, and burned and cleared the forest for farming.

Not only do animals and birds live in the forest, people live there as well. When the forest is destroyed, their land and homes are gone too.

There are over five billion people on the Earth and the number is growing all the time. In fact, there are 150 babies born across the world every minute!

Polluting the land, sea and air, killing the wildlife and destroying the forests affects every one of us. It upsets the delicate balance of nature on which we all depend.

A quarter of all the drugs and medicines prescribed by doctors come from plants found in the rainforest.

Rainforests contain half of all known types of wild creature.

No-one wants our planet to die, so everyone must work hard together to look after all life on Earth.

# The Weather

We have no way of controlling the weather. It changes all the time. Too much sunshine - not enough rain - storms and winds - frost and snow! These are all part of the Earth's weather and can change from hour to hour, or day to day.

## What makes the weather change?

As the heat of the Sun reaches Earth, it warms the air and makes it move around in the atmosphere. This causes the wind to blow, water vapour to rise and clouds to form to make rain and snow.

## What is atmosphere?

The Earth is covered with a layer of air called the atmosphere. As you move further away from the Earth the air gets thinner.

Near the ground breathing is easy. If you climb up a high mountain there is less oxygen, so it is harder to breathe. Higher up still, in an aeroplane, the air is so thin that the cabin is pressurised (air is pumped in) so that the passengers can breathe.

The atmosphere is a thick blanket of air wrapped round the Earth, protecting it from the fierce heat of the Sun by day, and keeping the warmth near the Earth at night.

**Mount Everest**

20

# It's the same old rain again!

All life on Earth depends on light from the Sun, but it also depends on an endless supply of water.

Did you know that the same old rain falls to Earth over and over again?

When warm winds blow over oceans or seas, the water on the top evaporates. This moisture then rises to form clouds in the sky.

As the clouds are blown over mountains or hills by the wind, they become cool. The moisture forms water droplets that fall to Earth as rain.

The rain runs into streams, then rivers and is carried back to the sea - to start all over again!

# Different clouds mean different weather

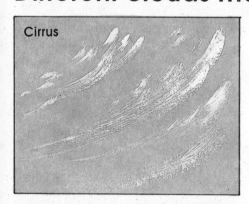

Cirrus

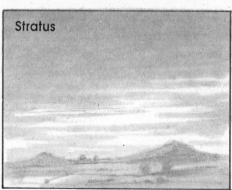

Stratus

Cumulus

Cumulonimbus

**Cirrus**
The highest clouds of all. Made of specks of ice, they have wispy, feathery shapes. Sometimes they are called 'mare's-tails'.

**Stratus**
Thin, low layers of grey cloud that often cover high ground. They usually bring drizzle.

**Cumulus**
Low, fluffy white clouds, like heaps of cotton wool that drift across the sky. They bring fine weather and sunny spells.

**Cumulonimbus**
Towering clouds like billowing smoke that reach high up into the sky. If the clouds are heavy and dark, a thunderstorm may be close by!

21

## Hailstones

Hailstones are raindrops that freeze as they fall through layers of very cold air.

When they fall down from the sky, hailstones are usually as big as peas. Sometimes they can be as big as tennis balls - so watch out!

## Snow

When water vapour in the clouds freezes it makes tiny ice crystals. These join together to form snowflakes.

If you look at a snowflake through a magnifying glass, you will see that most of these beautiful crystals form six-sided patterns. You will never find two the same - however hard you look!

## Fog

Fog is cloud that is near the ground instead of up in the sky. Damp air cools and hangs in the air. When the fog is thick, you can't see very well!

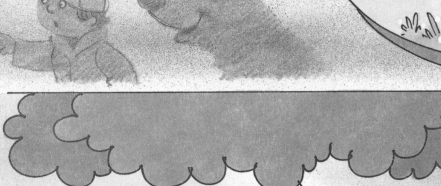

### Dew

On clear cloudless nights some of the Earth's warmth is lost in the atmosphere. The air near the ground cools and forms little drops of water that we call dew. If the temperature is below freezing the dew becomes frost.

## Lightning and thunder

Lightning is a huge electric spark passing between two clouds or travelling from a cloud to the Earth.

The loud crack of thunder we hear is the noise made by the giant spark, as the air expands round it.

Lightning and thunder happen at the same time, but you see the flash before you hear the thunder, because light travels faster than sound.

Tall trees and buildings are often struck by lightning. Never stand under a tree during a thunderstorm.

## Wind

Can you see the wind? Of course not! Wind is just air moving around. The wind can be a gentle breeze or a fierce hurricane blowing at a speed of 120 kph (75mph).

When the Earth's surface is warm, the air above it is heated and rises. Then cool air flows in to take its place. That movement of air is called wind.

## The Beaufort Scale

This was devised in 1806 by Admiral Beaufort of the British Royal Navy who used numbers to describe wind strengths.

When the weatherperson says 'force 9 on the Beaufort Scale', you know they mean a strong gale.

| Force | Strength | Kph | Force | Strength | Kph |
|-------|----------|-----|-------|----------|-----|
| 0 | Calm | 0-1 | 7 | Near Gale | 51-61 |
| 1 | Light air | 1-5 | 8 | Gale | 62-74 |
| 2 | Light breeze | 6-11 | 9 | Strong Gale | 75-87 |
| 3 | Gentle breeze | 12-19 | 10 | Storm | 88-101 |
| 4 | Moderate breeze | 20-29 | 11 | Violent storm | 102-117 |
| 5 | Fresh breeze | 30-39 | 12 | Hurricane | 118+ |
| 6 | Strong breeze | 40-50 | | | |

## How do we measure the weather?

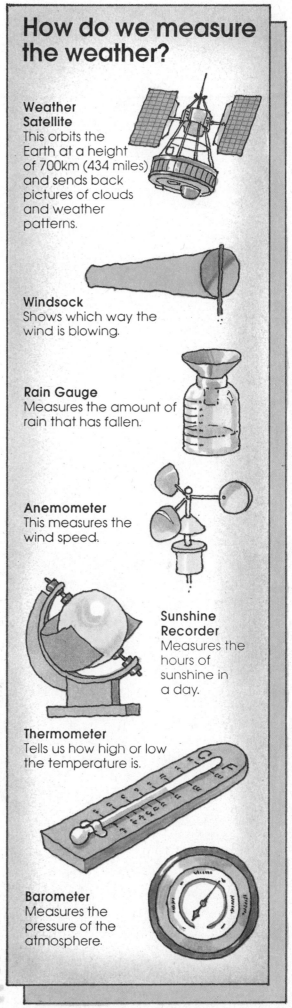

**Weather Satellite**
This orbits the Earth at a height of 700km (434 miles) and sends back pictures of clouds and weather patterns.

**Windsock**
Shows which way the wind is blowing.

**Rain Gauge**
Measures the amount of rain that has fallen.

**Anemometer**
This measures the wind speed.

**Sunshine Recorder**
Measures the hours of sunshine in a day.

**Thermometer**
Tells us how high or low the temperature is.

**Barometer**
Measures the pressure of the atmosphere.

# Life begins on Earth

Millions of years ago, the Earth was a mass of hot rocks and gases. As the Earth cooled, the huge cloud of steam that covered the planet turned to water. Then it fell as rain cooling the Earth even more and it made the rivers, seas and oceans.

Over many more millions of years the first forms of plant life began to grow in the sea. In time, simple animals evolved too - sponges, sea-snails and, eventually, fish.

Later on, plants started to grow by the edge of the water. Some sea creatures grew legs to walk on land and lungs to breathe in the air. Reptiles were the first creatures to breed on land, and some of the insects developed wings and could fly.

In Earth's warm steamy atmosphere, plants, insects and reptiles grew bigger and bigger - especially dinosaurs!

## The first out of the water

The first creatures to come out of the water were the lobe-finned fish that were developing lungs.

The first amphibian was the Ichthyostega that had strong legs for walking on land. It may have begun to leave the water searching for food in dry times.

Ichthyostega

# How do we know this happened?

The remains of plants, shells and bones of prehistoric creatures have been found millions of years later, preserved in stone. They are called fossils.

Fossils are found in layers of rock all over the world. The oldest ones are in the bottom layers, with the newer ones at the top.

Some fossils are quite small, such as a leaf preserved in rock. Others may be the whole skeleton of a dinosaur - the largest creature that ever walked on Earth!

Ammonites are common fossils which may be found on the seashore.

Many beautiful fossils are of leaves or plants.

Putting together bits of a creature no-one has ever seen before is like doing a jigsaw puzzle without the picture. Sometimes scientists must get it wrong!

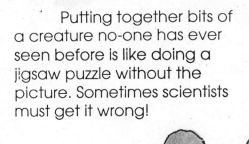

Finding a fossilised dinosaur skeleton is exciting work, especially to extract all the pieces from the rock in which they have lain for millions of years.

25

# The Dinosaurs

Although dinosaurs are now extinct, they lived all over the world for 160 million years. Human beings have lived on the Earth for just 35,000 years.

Some dinosaurs were huge creatures, the largest animals that ever walked the Earth. Others were small, not much bigger than a chicken!

**Deionosuchus**
Seventy-five million years ago this huge crocodile grew to a length of 16m (52ft).

**Euparkeria**
This chicken-sized dinosaur lived 245 million years ago. Although very small, it was a fast moving meat-eater.

**Dimetrodon**
This strange creature lived 285 million years ago. The sail on its back probably helped to control body temperature. At 3.5m (11ft) in length, it was a predator feeding on smaller animals.

**Dryosaurus**
This plant-eater was 3m (10ft) long and would need all of its speed to avoid the allosaurus.

**Allosaurus**
At 13m (43ft) long and weighing over two tonnes, this fierce meat-eater was definitely one to avoid 200 million years ago.

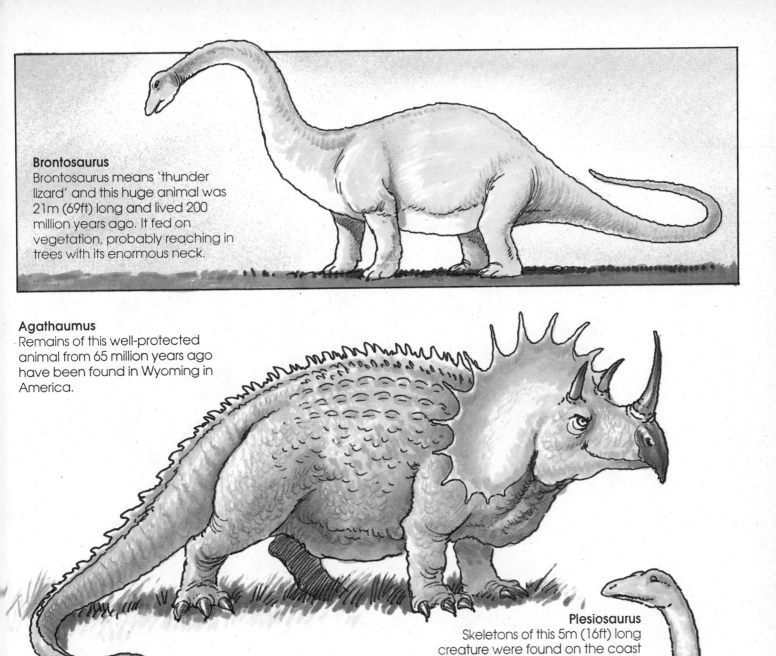

**Brontosaurus**
Brontosaurus means 'thunder lizard' and this huge animal was 21m (69ft) long and lived 200 million years ago. It fed on vegetation, probably reaching in trees with its enormous neck.

**Agathaumus**
Remains of this well-protected animal from 65 million years ago have been found in Wyoming in America.

**Plesiosaurus**
Skeletons of this 5m (16ft) long creature were found on the coast of England over 200 years ago. Many people believe that this is the famous Loch Ness monster from Scotland, although it lived over 200 million years ago.

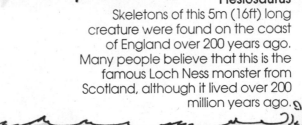

**Ichthyosaurus**
Dolphin-like, but much bigger at 10m (33ft), this fish-eater roamed the seas 225 million years ago.

27

## Deinonychus
The name means 'terrible claw'. Although only as tall as a man, this fast moving hunter had a terrible weapon - a 12cm (4½") claw on the first toe of each foot that it would use to disembowel its prey.

## Archaeopteryx
This feathered dinosaur was probably the ancestor of the birds. About the size of a crow, this creature lived in the Jurassic period 195-135 million years ago.

## Tyrannosaurus Rex
The king of the dinosaurs! This giant beast lived about 100 million years ago. It stood 5m (16ft) tall and 14m (45ft) long. Rather than killing its own prey it survived by frightening smaller dinosaurs from their kill.

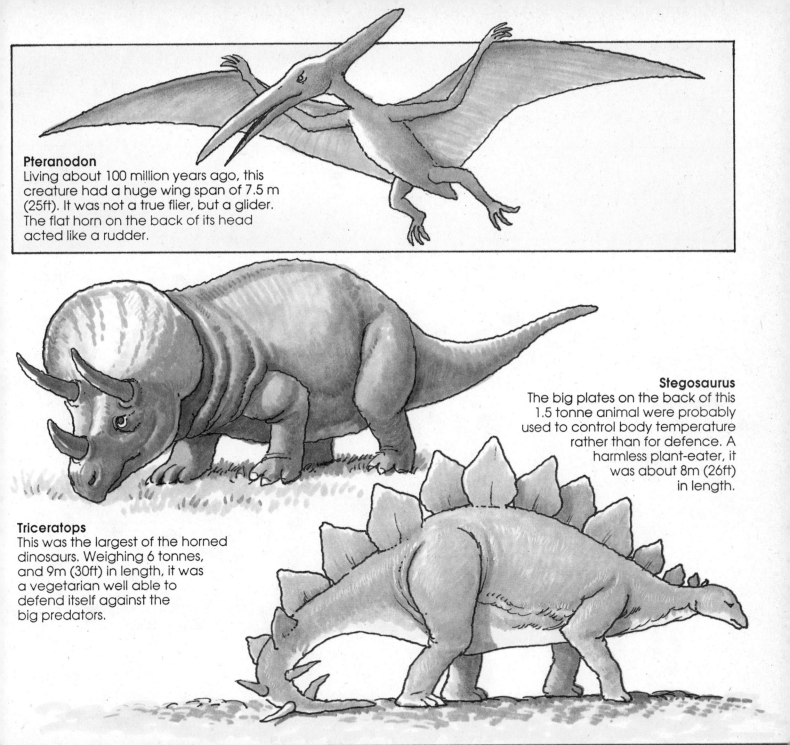

### Pteranodon

Living about 100 million years ago, this creature had a huge wing span of 7.5 m (25ft). It was not a true flier, but a glider. The flat horn on the back of its head acted like a rudder.

### Stegosaurus

The big plates on the back of this 1.5 tonne animal were probably used to control body temperature rather than for defence. A harmless plant-eater, it was about 8m (26ft) in length.

### Triceratops

This was the largest of the horned dinosaurs. Weighing 6 tonnes, and 9m (30ft) in length, it was a vegetarian well able to defend itself against the big predators.

# Why did the dinosaurs die out?

Dinosaurs roamed the Earth for about 160 million years. Then about 65 million years ago they vanished. No-one really knows why.

Some scientists think that a huge meteor hit the Earth and started volcanic eruptions - the dust and ash would have blotted out the Sun for years. Or perhaps the Earth's climate grew much colder and the cold-blooded dinosaurs could not stand the cold as well as the warm-blooded mammals that had begun to live on Earth.

"I don't think I would like to have met this one."

# Plants

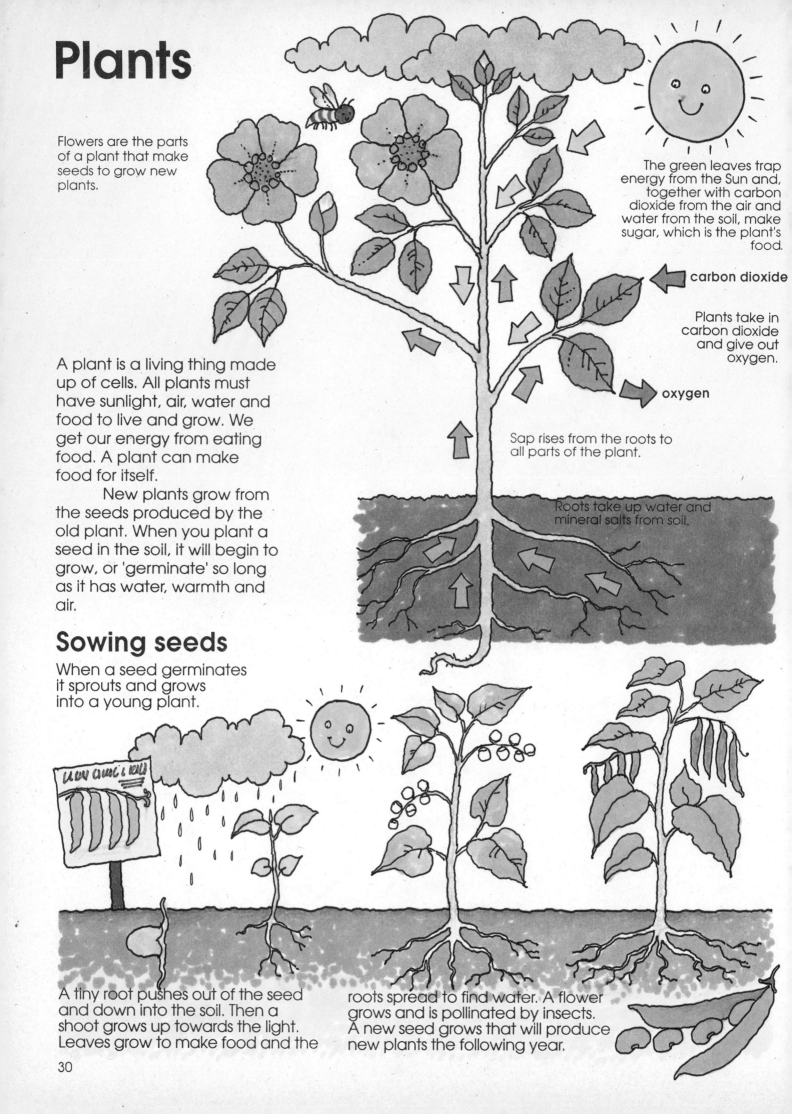

Flowers are the parts of a plant that make seeds to grow new plants.

The green leaves trap energy from the Sun and, together with carbon dioxide from the air and water from the soil, make sugar, which is the plant's food.

**carbon dioxide**

Plants take in carbon dioxide and give out oxygen.

**oxygen**

A plant is a living thing made up of cells. All plants must have sunlight, air, water and food to live and grow. We get our energy from eating food. A plant can make food for itself.

New plants grow from the seeds produced by the old plant. When you plant a seed in the soil, it will begin to grow, or 'germinate' so long as it has water, warmth and air.

Sap rises from the roots to all parts of the plant.

Roots take up water and mineral salts from soil.

## Sowing seeds

When a seed germinates it sprouts and grows into a young plant.

A tiny root pushes out of the seed and down into the soil. Then a shoot grows up towards the light. Leaves grow to make food and the roots spread to find water. A flower grows and is pollinated by insects. A new seed grows that will produce new plants the following year.

# What is a flower?

The flower is very important because it produces the seeds for the new plant. Insects are very important to the flower.

As insects move from flower to flower to drink the nectar, the flower's dusty pollen sticks to them and falls on the next flower that the insect visits.

This pollinates the flower to make seeds.

Petal

Stamen with pollen

Stigma

Eggs

Sepal

"We're off to page 36 to join the other insects."

## Scattering seeds

Some seeds just drop from the plant to the ground. Here are some plants that have more unusual ways of spreading their seeds.

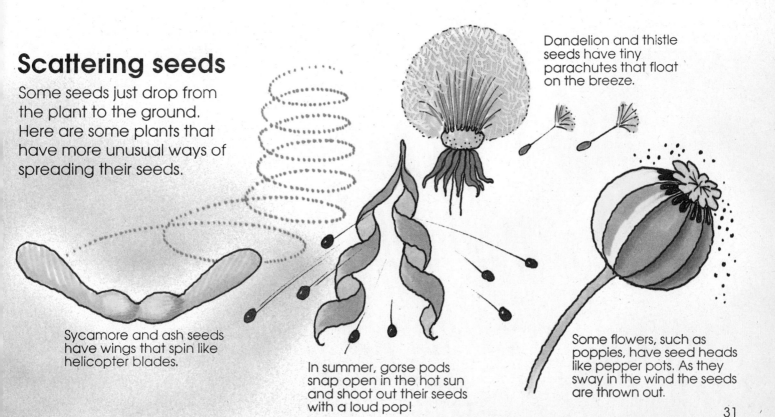

Dandelion and thistle seeds have tiny parachutes that float on the breeze.

Sycamore and ash seeds have wings that spin like helicopter blades.

In summer, gorse pods snap open in the hot sun and shoot out their seeds with a loud pop!

Some flowers, such as poppies, have seed heads like pepper pots. As they sway in the wind the seeds are thrown out.

31

# Fungi and Cacti

Fungi come in many different shapes and sizes. They grow as mushrooms in fields and also as fluffy grey mould on stale food.

Fungi cannot make their own food like other plants. Instead they get a ready made food supply by growing on other plants or decaying matter, like rotting wood or dead leaves.

Fungi have no flowers or seeds, they scatter fine spores just like the fern group of plants.

Although some fungi, such as the mushroom can be eaten, many are poisonous. It is safer to leave them alone!

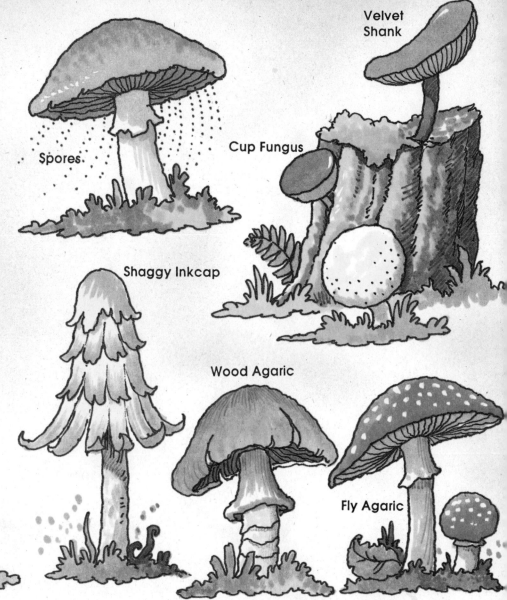

Spores.

Velvet Shank

Cup Fungus

Shaggy Inkcap

Wood Agaric

Fly Agaric

Fairy Ring Mushroom

Most plants cannot survive in the hot, dry desert. There is not enough water in the soil to replace the moisture lost through their leaves.

The cactus plants are able to store water in the fleshy parts within their thick, tough skins. No water is lost through their leaves which are the prickly spikes like needles. These also protect the plant from animals seeking moisture.

Cacti produce beautiful flowers, but they do so very rarely, sometimes only once in their lifetime - just enough to produce their seeds.

Giant Saguaro grows up to 18m (60ft) tall

32

# Plants we eat

Much of the food we eat comes from plants. There are many different plants that are eaten all over the world.

The group of plants known as cereals are grown so that their seeds can be gathered, or harvested as grain, which is the world's main food.

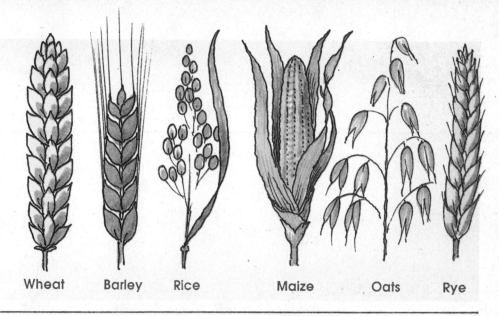

Wheat  Barley  Rice  Maize  Oats  Rye

Vegetables - we eat the roots of the carrot, turnip and potato; the leaves of cabbages, lettuce and broccoli; and the leaf stalks of celery, leeks and onions. Dried peas, beans and lentils are pulses, and are full of protein.

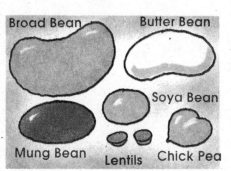

Broad Bean  Butter Bean
Soya Bean
Mung Bean  Lentils  Chick Pea

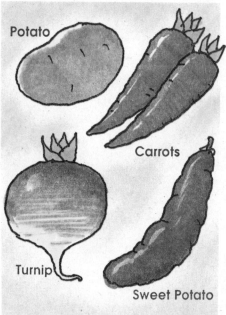

Potato
Carrots
Turnip
Sweet Potato

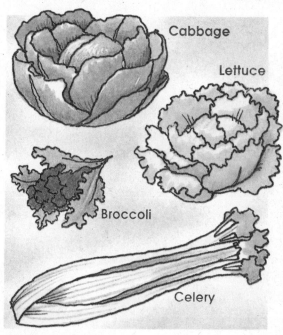

Cabbage
Lettuce
Broccoli
Celery

Fruits - contain the seeds of flowering plants. A peach has one seed, a melon has hundreds. Oranges and lemons are citrus fruits that grow on evergreen shrubs in warm lands.

Melon
Grapes
Lemon  Lime
Strawberry
Pear
Apple
Peach
Orange
Blueberries
Blackberry
Banana

33

# Trees

Trees can grow larger and live longer than any other living thing on Earth. The giant sequoia can reach over 100 metres (328ft) and live for over 3,000 years. It is the world's tallest tree.

A tree grows very slowly, upwards and outwards. The roots spread out underground, some deep in the ground and others near the surface.

However large the tree, it still grew from a seed just as smaller plants do.

Deciduous trees with broad fat leaves stop growing in the cold weather. They do not need their leaves to trap sunlight or give off moisture, so they shed them as winter approaches.

Evergreen trees have tough, thin leaves like needles that lose very little water. They do not shed their leaves in winter, they stay 'ever green'.

Trees like the pine and fir keep their seeds hidden inside beautiful cones.

Acorns are the seeds of the mighty oak.

Trees come in many shapes and sizes, here are some well known ones:

**Flowering cherry** grow to 6m (20ft) in height

**Lemon** 7m (22ft)

**Apple** 10m (33ft)

**Laurel** 20m (66ft)

**Weeping Willow** 22m (72ft)

**Yew** 25m (82ft)

# The Kings Of The Forest

Each year as a tree grows, it adds a new ring of wood beneath the bark. When a tree is cut down you can find out its age by counting the rings.

Imagine the history in the rings of the great sequoia over 3,000 years old:

**1981** Launch of space shuttle 'Columbia'

**1969** First man on the Moon

**1939** Second World War began

**1914** First World War began

**1903** First flight in aeroplane

The most massive sequoia 'General Sherman' is so far round (25m, 82ft) that a human being would only look this big stood against a slice of it.

Stonehenge built when the tree was a seedling

**753BC** City of Rome founded

**55BC** Roman invasion of Britain

**0** Birth of Jesus Christ

**570** Birth of Mohammed

**868** First printed book in China

**1492** Columbus sails for the New World

**1564** Birth of William Shakespeare

**1620** The 'Mayflower' reaches America

**1805** Battle of Trafalgar

**1876** Telephone invented by Alexander Graham Bell

**1887** First successful motor car

| Beech | Poplar | Scots Pine | Oak | Larch | Douglas Fir |
|-------|--------|-----------|-----|-------|-------------|
| 30m (98ft) | 35m (115ft) | 35m (115ft) | 35m (115ft) | 40m (131ft) | 50m+ (164ft+) |

# Insects

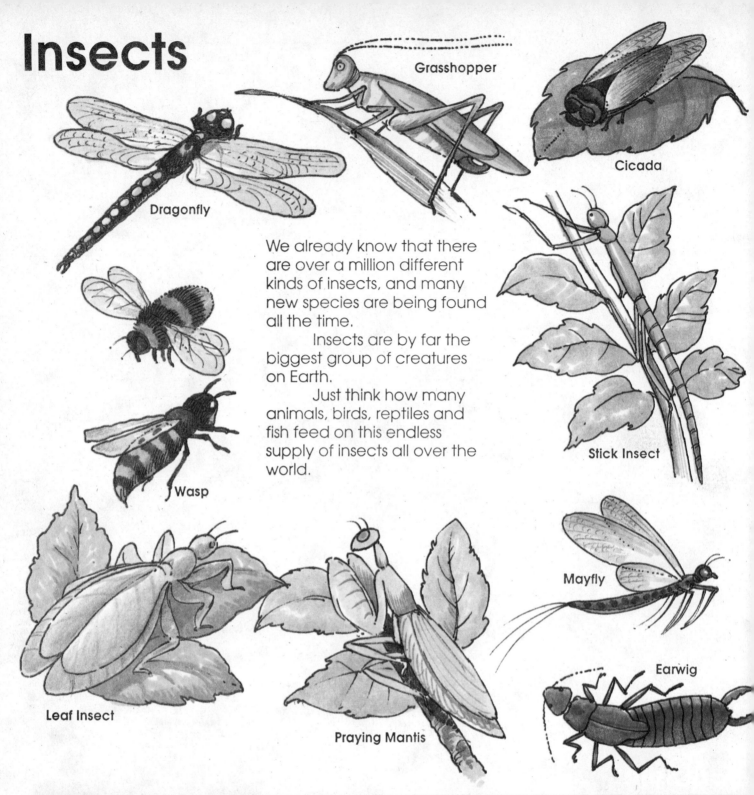

Grasshopper

Cicada

Dragonfly

Wasp

Stick Insect

We already know that there are over a million different kinds of insects, and many new species are being found all the time.

Insects are by far the biggest group of creatures on Earth.

Just think how many animals, birds, reptiles and fish feed on this endless supply of insects all over the world.

Leaf Insect

Praying Mantis

Mayfly

Earwig

## What is an insect?

An insect is a creature without a backbone and with a body divided into three main parts: the head, thorax and abdomen.

Most insects have three pairs of legs and one or two pairs of wings.

The 'feelers' or antennae on the insect's head are its sense of touch and smell.

Some insects have a sting in the abdomen.

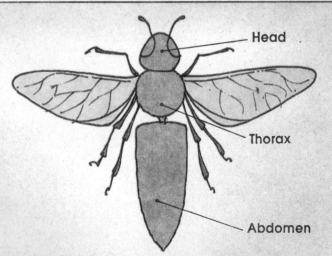

Head

Thorax

Abdomen

36

# Beetles

Most beetles have two pairs of wings. Underneath the first hard pair on the beetle's back is another delicate pair. You can see these as the beetle flies around.

When the beetle lands, the second pair fold away. The first pair then close down like a shell to protect them.

Ladybird

Phosphorus Virescens

Colorado Beetle

Rhinoceros Beetle

Stag Beetle

Asparagus Beetle

Goliath Beetle

Sack Beetle

Sternodes Caspieus

# Ants and Termites

Ants live together in large colonies and often make nests underground.

The ant hill is full of passages and separate cells for eggs and food.

Worker ants build the nests, gather food and look after the larvae that hatch from the eggs, until they turn into young ants.

Termites are ant-like insects. They build huge mounds of earth from grains of soil.

Inside live millions of termites in tunnels and chambers. Some mounds are over eight metres (26ft) high.

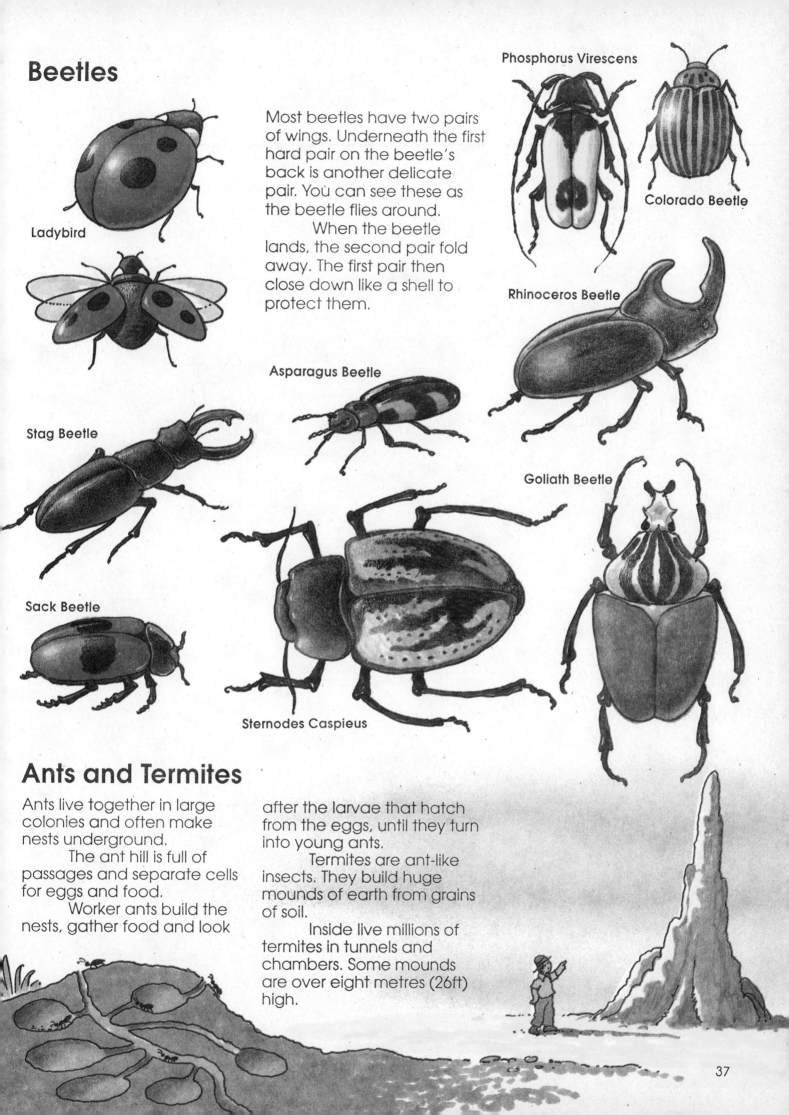

37

# Butterflies

A butterfly begins life as an egg. The egg hatches and out comes a caterpillar. The caterpillar grows, shedding its skin several times. At full size it becomes a pupa in a hard shell. After a while the shell cracks open and out squeezes a new butterfly.

Butterflies love the sunshine. If you walk in a garden on a sunny day, you will often find beautiful butterflies feeding on the nectar of bright flowers and blossoms.

Their lovely colours are made up of millions of minute scales that overlap one after another and cover the wings. These can only be seen through a microscope, as they are as fine as dust. Butterflies shouldn't be picked up as this rubs off the scales, making flight difficult.

Egg          Caterpillar          Pupa          Butterfly

Large Blue

Monarch

Ulysses

Large Copper

Green Hairstreak resting with wings folded.

Brimstone

Small Tortoiseshell

# Moths

Butterflies and moths look very much alike, but moths usually fly by night and rest by day.

When a butterfly rests, its wings are closed and held straight up, while a moth keeps its wings spread out flat.

Moths are not usually as colourful as butterflies, and their bodies have a fatter shape.

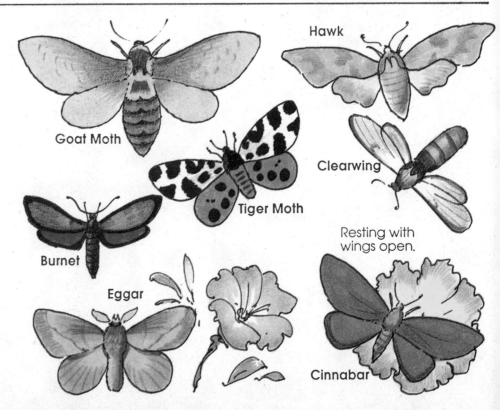

Hawk

Goat Moth

Clearwing

Tiger Moth

Burnet

Resting with wings open.

Eggar

Cinnabar

# Bees

Bees do an important job for all the plant life of this planet.

As they fly from flower to flower collecting nectar, dusty pollen clings to their legs and bodies. This pollinates the flowers so that they will produce seeds.

# What a pest!

Some insects do a great deal of harm. They can destroy crops and spread sickness and disease. We call these insects pests!

Flies can be a danger to health - they breed in refuse and carry germs on their feet that they can transfer to any food that is uncovered.

Locusts are a type of grasshopper. In the tropics they swarm in search of food, often travelling over 1,000km (621 miles). When a swarm lands, the insects eat vast quantities of crops and food, which causes famine in some lands.

Mosquitoes can be a serious pest in tropical countries, because they spread a sickness called malaria. They feed by piercing the skin, then sucking out the blood. This infects the wound with germs and spreads the disease.

# Is a spider an insect?

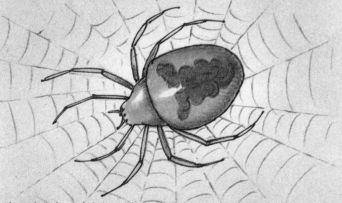

Look at a spider. You will see it has eight legs and its body is divided into two parts. This means it is not an insect! It is an arachnid and belongs to the same family as the scorpion.

The spider spins a sticky, silk thread, then builds a web to catch insects. When the spider feels the web move, it knows it has caught a meal!

The scorpion lives in hot, dry countries. It waits with its claws open to catch its prey.

Sometimes the scorpion uses the sting at the top of its tail to paralyse large insects it cannot catch with its claws.

# Birds

Birds are warm-blooded creatures. Their bodies are covered in feathers that help to keep them warm and dry. There are over 8,600 different kinds of birds in the world. They all have wings - but not all of them can fly!

All birds lay eggs, inside which young birds develop. When a baby bird grows too big for its egg, it chips a hole in the shell from inside, and very soon hatches out.

## Feathers and flight

Because birds fly, their bodies are designed to be as light as possible. Their feathers weigh very little, they have no teeth and their beaks are made of horn. Although their bones are hollow, they are strong and light.

## Eggs and nests

Baby birds that hatch in a nest start off life blind and featherless. They must be fed and kept warm for several weeks by their parents until they are ready to fly.

Other chicks that hatch out in nests on the ground or near water have fluffy down feathers and they are soon able to run around and find food. Some can even swim.

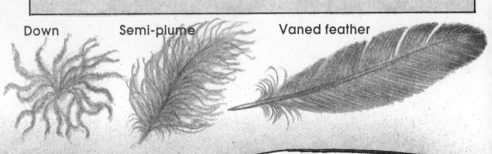

Down          Semi-plume          Vaned feather

An albatross uses its huge wing span to glide great distances over the ocean.

The kingfisher folds its wings and dives straight into the water to spear fish on its sharp beak.

Most birds have a streamlined shape that helps them to fly. Their wings are like strong arms that lift the bird into the air, then propel it along.

A bird can change the shape or angle of its wings to change course. Together with the tail, wings help the bird to steer, brake and land.

The tiny humming bird can beat its wings at great speed. It can also hover in mid-air and even fly backwards.

Many water birds have to run along the surface to gain speed before lifting off.

## Birds that cannot fly

Of the thousands of types of birds, only a small number cannot fly. This group includes the heaviest and the largest birds - the ostrich, emu, cassowary and penguin.

Penguin

Takahe

Kiwi

Cassowary

Ostrich

## Fruit and seed eaters

**Toucan** - lives on soft fruit.

**Parrot** - eats fruit and nuts.

**Quail** - eats mainly grass seeds.

**Crossbill** - picks the seed from pine cones.

41

# Swimmers

Some birds are able to swim because they have slightly oily, waterproof feathers. All of the swimmers have broad, webbed feet that act like paddles. They get food such as fish, snails and plants from the water.

Puffin

Herring Gull

Canada Goose

Mute Swan

Black-necked Grebe

Teal

# Waders

These water birds are not able to swim, they live on the water's edge. They all have long beaks and legs, and wade out into the water in search of food.

Spoonbill

Heron

Flamingo

42

# Insect eaters

Most of the insect eaters are small, fast moving birds with sharp beaks. Some, like the swallow, catch their food in mid-air.

Woodpecker

Bee-eater

Red-backed Shrike

Swallow

# Birds of Prey

These large birds catch and kill their food with their strong beaks and claws. They have very good eyesight that enables them to see any small movement on the ground.

Bald Eagle

Monkey-eating Eagle

Peregrine Falcon

Long-eared Owl

Vulture

# Life in the seas and oceans

Bottle-nosed Dolphin

Turtle

Jellyfish

Seal

Killer Whale

Tuna

Thresher Shark

Coelacanth

Viperfish

## The ocean depths
The bottom of the ocean is a cold and dark place. No plants grow because there is no sunlight. There are very few fish, and because food is scarce many have developed huge, wide-open mouths to snap up anything they come across. Some have developed lights as lures to catch their prey.

There are countless numbers of creatures that make their home in the sea, from the microscopic plankton that drift near the surface, to the largest creature on Earth, the blue whale.

There are brightly coloured tropical fish that swim around the coral reefs, and strange-looking fish that live in the darkness of the ocean bed.

All are part of the endless variety of life that is found in our seas and oceans.

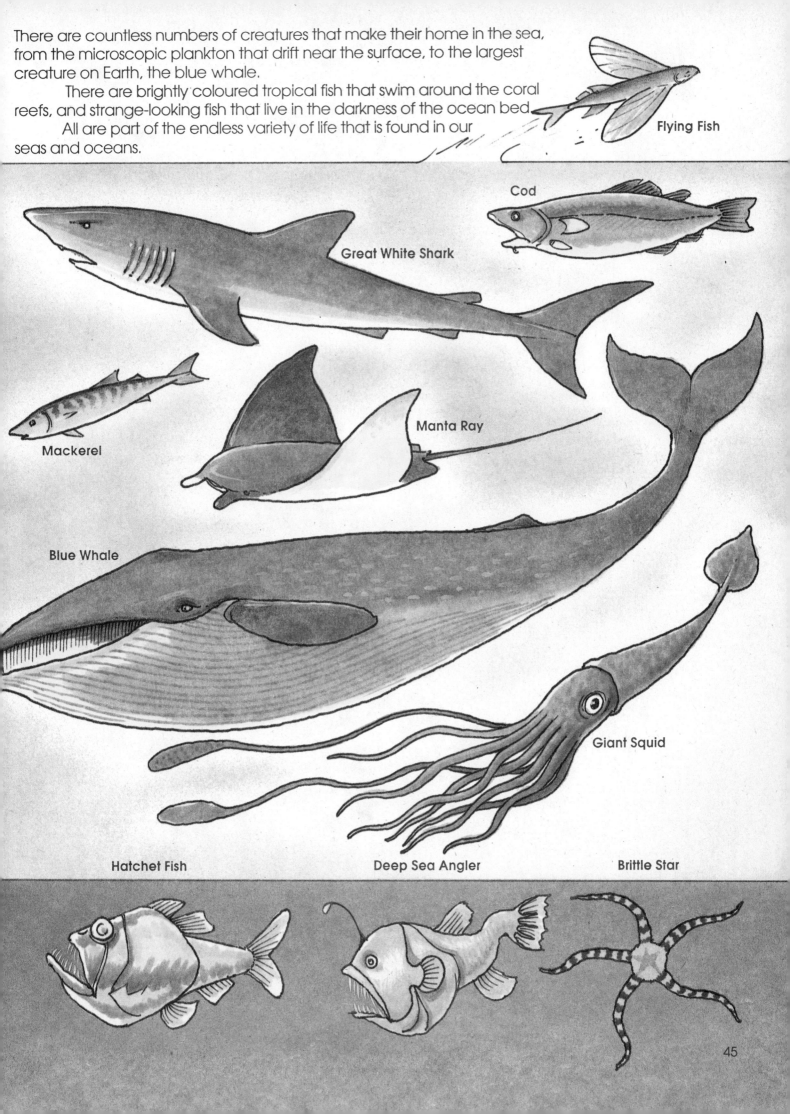

Flying Fish

Cod

Great White Shark

Mackerel

Manta Ray

Blue Whale

Giant Squid

Hatchet Fish

Deep Sea Angler

Brittle Star

45

# How a fish breathes

Fish breathe by taking oxygen from the water. They take the water in through their mouths, pass it over their gills, which extract the oxygen. Then the water is pushed out of the gill slits.

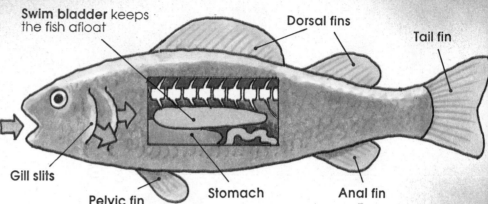

**Swim bladder** keeps the fish afloat

Dorsal fins

Tail fin

Gill slits

Pelvic fin

Stomach

Anal fin

# The world's biggest fish

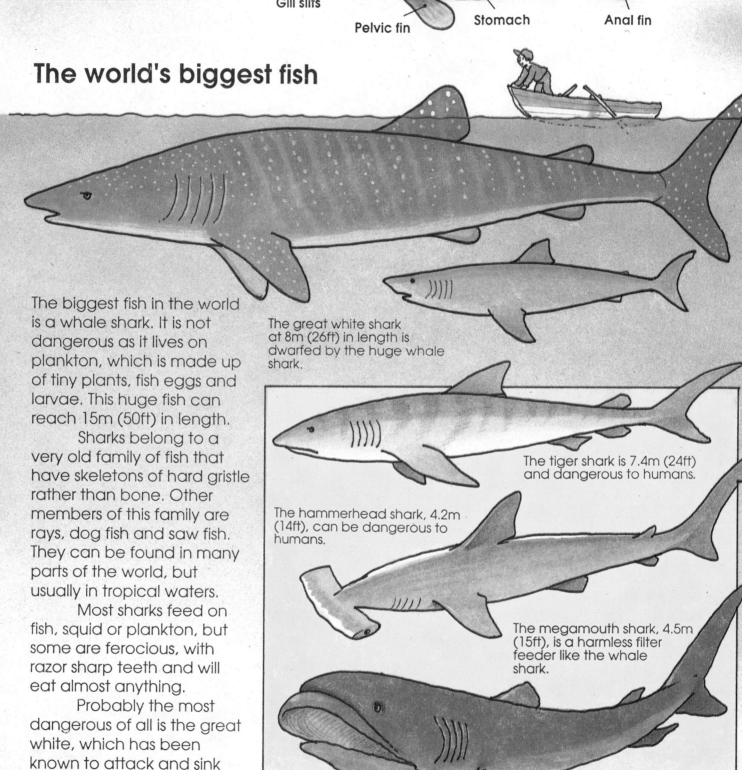

The biggest fish in the world is a whale shark. It is not dangerous as it lives on plankton, which is made up of tiny plants, fish eggs and larvae. This huge fish can reach 15m (50ft) in length.

Sharks belong to a very old family of fish that have skeletons of hard gristle rather than bone. Other members of this family are rays, dog fish and saw fish. They can be found in many parts of the world, but usually in tropical waters.

Most sharks feed on fish, squid or plankton, but some are ferocious, with razor sharp teeth and will eat almost anything.

Probably the most dangerous of all is the great white, which has been known to attack and sink small boats.

The great white shark at 8m (26ft) in length is dwarfed by the huge whale shark.

The tiger shark is 7.4m (24ft) and dangerous to humans.

The hammerhead shark, 4.2m (14ft), can be dangerous to humans.

The megamouth shark, 4.5m (15ft), is a harmless filter feeder like the whale shark.

# Life on a coral reef

Coral is a type of chalky rock. It is made up of the hard skeletons and the living bodies of millions of tiny coral animals that live in warm shallow tropical seas. Coral exists in many different shapes and colours.

After many years the corals knit together to form huge ridges or reefs. The Great Barrier Reef off the coast of Australia is 2,000 km (1,250 miles) long.

Sometimes the coral builds up to form islands and circular reefs called atolls. A coral reef is home to countless beautiful and unusual fish and plants.

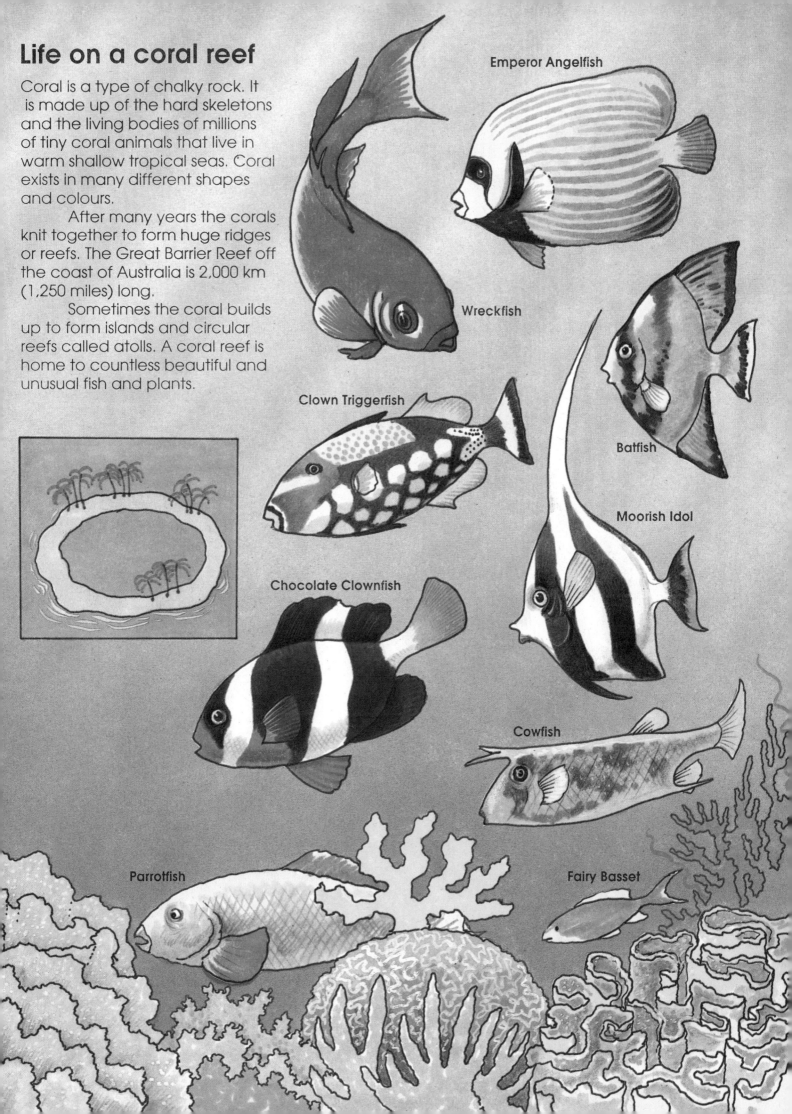

Emperor Angelfish

Wreckfish

Batfish

Clown Triggerfish

Moorish Idol

Chocolate Clownfish

Cowfish

Parrotfish

Fairy Basset

# Amphibians

Amphibians begin their life in water. At first they breathe through gills, then their lungs develop, enabling them to live on land. They must return to the water to breed.

Frogs lay many eggs in water. Tadpoles hatch and, after a while, they grow legs and lungs. The last stage is to shed their tails before they become frogs.

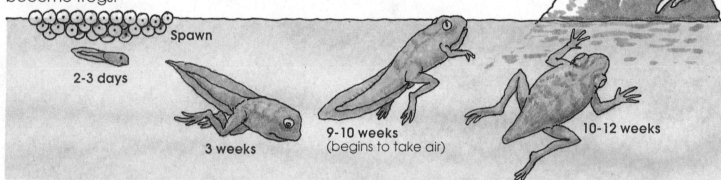

Spawn

2-3 days

3 weeks

9-10 weeks
(begins to take air)

10-12 weeks

Toad

Salamander

Newt

# Reptiles

In prehistoric times there were great numbers of strange reptiles, but most of them are extinct now.

The reptiles we know today include snakes, crocodiles and alligators, tortoises and turtles, and lizards. They are cold-blooded and produce their young from eggs. Their skins are usually scaly.

The turtle has flippers and lives in the sea. It is related to the tortoise, which lives on land.

**European Tortoise**

**Giant Tortoise** of the Galapagos Islands can live over 100 years.

**Green Turtles** swim in the warm seas around Australia.

**The Giant Leatherback Turtle** of the Pacific Ocean is over 2m (6ft 6").

# Crocodiles and Alligators

These reptiles usually live in the lakes and rivers of hot countries, but they crawl up onto the bank to bask in the sunshine. They feed on fish and often grab larger animals, which they tear apart and eat in the water.

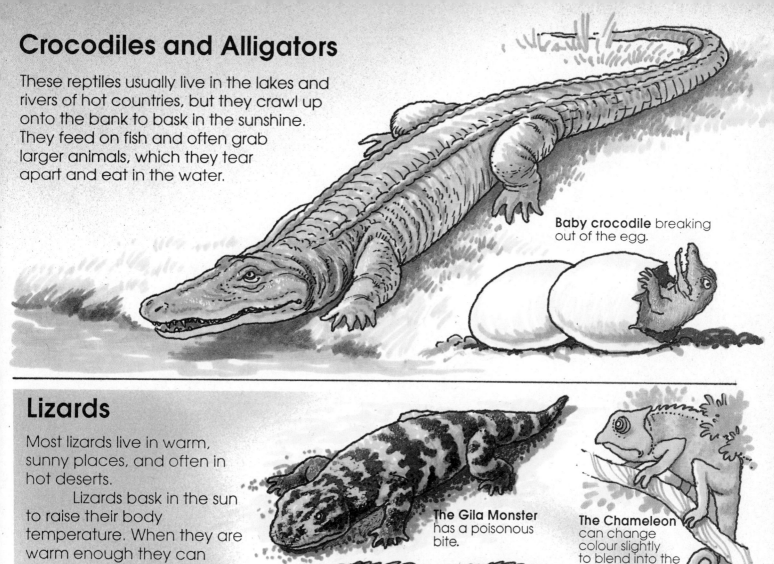

**Baby crocodile** breaking out of the egg.

# Lizards

Most lizards live in warm, sunny places, and often in hot deserts.

Lizards bask in the sun to raise their body temperature. When they are warm enough they can move about quickly to search for food. As their body temperature drops, lizards slow down.

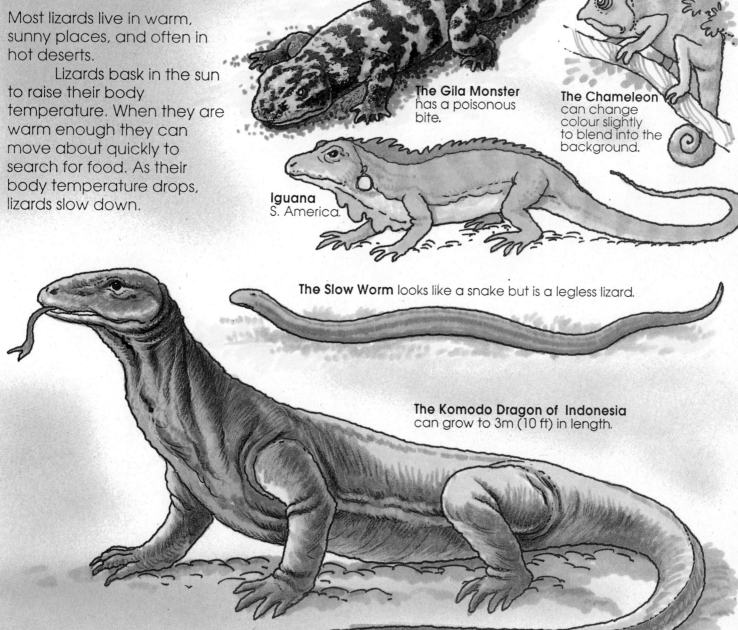

**The Gila Monster** has a poisonous bite.

**The Chameleon** can change colour slightly to blend into the background.

**Iguana** S. America.

**The Slow Worm** looks like a snake but is a legless lizard.

**The Komodo Dragon of Indonesia** can grow to 3m (10 ft) in length.

49

# Snakes

Snakes are limbless reptiles that can vary a great deal in size and colour, but very little in shape. A snake can shed its scaly skin completely as it grows.

Many snakes are harmless, but others such as the cobra and rattlesnake kill their prey with venom.

Snakes do not chew their food, but swallow it whole. The lower jaw is in two halves and can stretch sideways so the snake can swallow larger animals than itself.

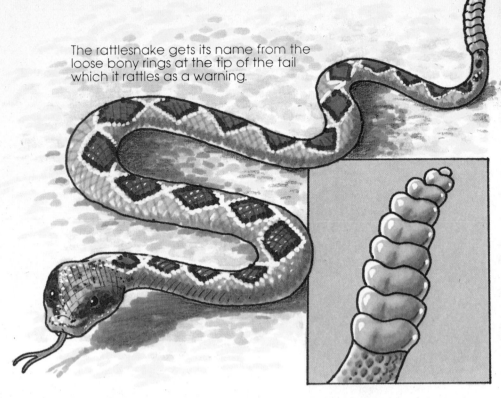

The rattlesnake gets its name from the loose bony rings at the tip of the tail which it rattles as a warning.

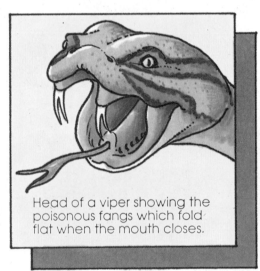

Head of a viper showing the poisonous fangs which fold flat when the mouth closes.

King Cobra

The body of the sea snake is flattened for swimming. It lives in the warm Indian and Pacific Oceans and eats fish and eels. The world's most posionous sea snake lives off the coast of north Australia.

The boa and pythons kill their prey by constriction (crushing), rather than poison. They wrap themselves round their prey, usually a small animal or bird, and squeeze!

The largest of the boas is the anaconda of S. America, which can be over 6m (20ft) in length.

# Mammals

Mammals are warm-blooded creatures. All of them have backbones, and some grow hair or fur on their bodies to keep warm. They feed their young on milk produced by the mother.

Humans are mammals. Our babies, like all other mammals, are born as living creatures. There are two animals found in Australia that are very different. They are the only two egg-laying mammals in the world!

## Platypus

This strange animal is part-reptile and part-mammal, with a duck-bill and webbed feet. The female platypus lays her eggs in a nest at the end of a long burrow. She hatches them with her warm furry body, then feeds her young with her milk.

## Echidna

This animal is also known as the spiny anteater. It has a coat of sharp spines, a long beak and a sticky tongue. This is used to reach into the nests of termites and ants for food. The female echidna has a pouch in which she puts her eggs. Then she feeds her young with milk when they hatch.

## Animals with pouches

Koala Bear

Wombat

Honey Possom

Brush-tail Possom

Kangaroo

# A world of difference

There are around 4,500 types of mammal and they behave in their own special way, and have their own unique lifestyle. Some mammals live in trees, many underground, while others live in the sea. Some can run very fast, others move slowly. Several can glide, but only one mammal - the bat - can fly. To survive, every mammal must find food, escape from danger and bring up its young.

Bats live in groups that hunt by night, while by day they hang upside-down to rest. Most bats eat insects that they find by a kind of bat radar. A bat sends out high-pitched squeaks as it flies. This wave of sound travels in front of the bat. When it hits anything in its path the sound wave bounces back rather like an echo and this is picked up by the bat's sensitive ears. Others eat fruit and a few feed on blood.

# Furry gliders

These mammals glide from one tree to another. As they jump they stretch out all four legs. They have flaps of skin on either side of their body that they spread out to form a type of parachute.

When gliding, the tail is used as a rudder to steer.

**European Flying Squirrel**

**Australian Sugar Glider**

# Mammals that live in the sea

Although whales, dolphins and porpoises live in the sea, they are mammals rather than fish. Mammals must have air, and all these sea creatures come to the surface to breathe.

Some whales, such as the sperm whale, the narwhal, porpoises and dolphins, have teeth and feed on fish and squid.

Others like the bowhead, the blue whale and the fin whale have no teeth. They feed on tiny sea creatures by straining the water through strips of whalebone, called baleen, that hang like sieves in their mouths.

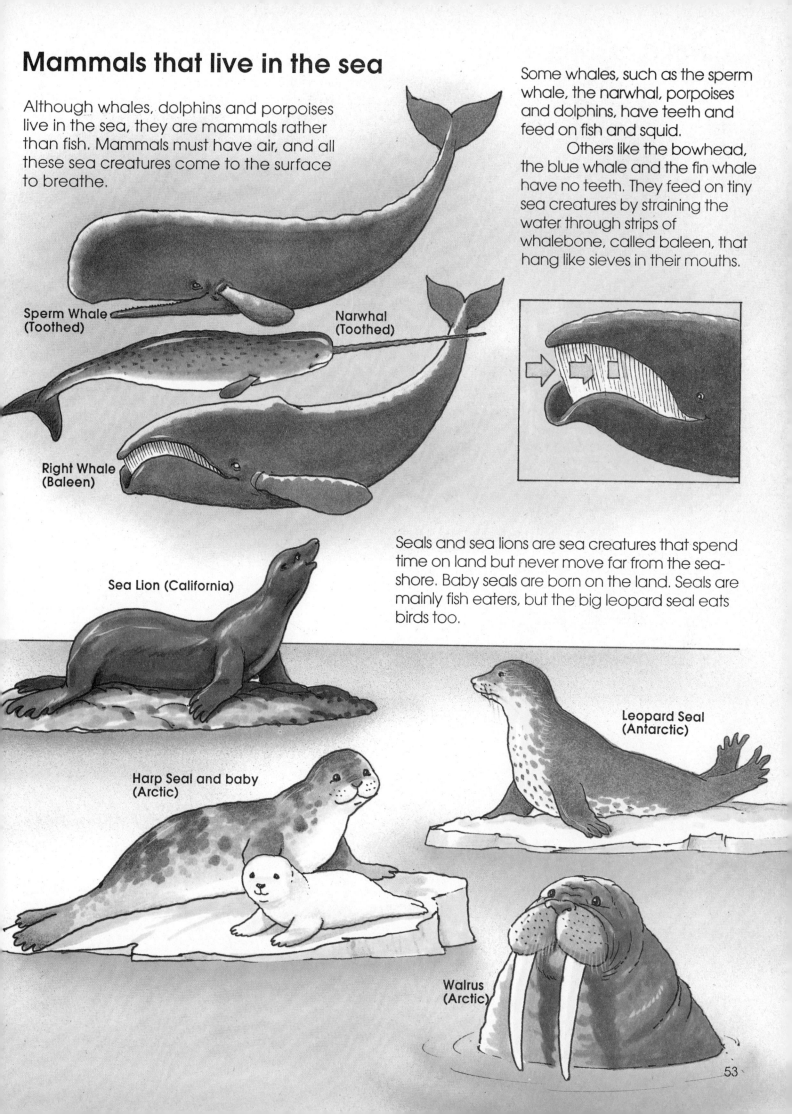

**Sperm Whale (Toothed)**

**Narwhal (Toothed)**

**Right Whale (Baleen)**

Seals and sea lions are sea creatures that spend time on land but never move far from the sea-shore. Baby seals are born on the land. Seals are mainly fish eaters, but the big leopard seal eats birds too.

**Sea Lion (California)**

**Leopard Seal (Antarctic)**

**Harp Seal and baby (Arctic)**

**Walrus (Arctic)**

53

# Grazing animals

Many mammals are plant eaters. Some graze on grass while others are tall with long necks or trunks that are perfect for reaching leaves high up in the trees.

In Africa, great areas of grassland are home to a huge variety of mammals. Some live together in great herds, often travelling long distances together in search of food and water.

They must always be on the look-out for predators. Predators are the meat-eating animals that hunt the grazing animals and kill them for food.

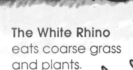

**Elephants** like to eat the highest leaves, but cause a lot of damage to the tree.

**The White Rhino** eats coarse grass and plants.

**The Wildebeest** eats the tops of sweet grasses, the herd is always on the move.

**Zebras** eat the coarser grasses and stalks.

# The predators

**The Lion** is the greatest of the predators in Africa. It is the female that usually makes the kill.

**Cheetah**
The world's fastest animal uses its great speed, 113kph (70mph), to catch small antelope.

54

**Sable Antelope**
This handsome animal with great curved horns is a grass eater.

**Impala**
Another of the grass eating antelopes of the African plains.

**The Giraffe**
eats the leaves from the highest part of the tree.

**Kudu**
This large antelope eats the lower leaves of the acacia tree.

**The Gerenuk**
reaches high in the tree by standing on its hind legs.

**Thomson's Gazelle**
This pretty little animal eats young grass shoots.

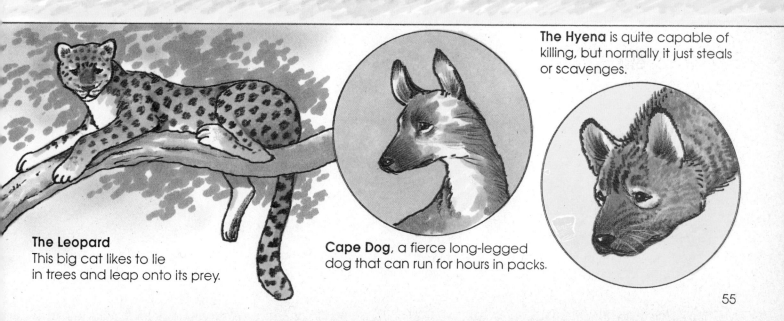

**The Hyena** is quite capable of killing, but normally it just steals or scavenges.

**The Leopard**
This big cat likes to lie in trees and leap onto its prey.

**Cape Dog**, a fierce long-legged dog that can run for hours in packs.

# Monkeys and Apes

Monkeys belong to the group of mammals called primates which includes apes and humans. They live mostly in trees and are found in tropical and subtropical countries.

The monkeys of S. America (the new world) are different to their cousins in Africa and Asia (the old world) as they have prehensile tails, that is, tails that can grip like a third hand.

Most monkeys are harmless, many small types such as the marmosets can be kept as pets. One group that are not very friendly are the baboons. Large and dog-like, they can be very dangerous. The mandrill is one of these.

**The new world**

Monkeys of the new world (the Americas) have 'prehensile' tails, which means they can grip like an extra limb.

Howler Monkey

Lion Tamarin

Capuchin

**The old world**

Red Colobus - Africa

Proboscis Monkey - Borneo

Mandrill - African rainforest

## The Great Apes

These are our nearest relatives in the animal world. They are the gibbon and orangutan of Borneo and Sumatra, and the chimpanzee and gorilla of Africa. None have tails.

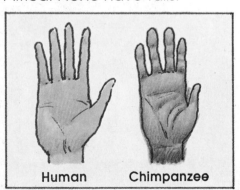

Human          Chimpanzee

Mountain Gorilla - Africa

Chimpanzee

# Early humans

It is possible that ape-like creatures living over 10 million years ago were human beings' early ancestors. Over millions of years they began to look more like us, they could make fire and use simple tools.

The first true humans appeared about 2 million years ago. Scientists called them Homo Habilis or 'Handy Man' because they could make stone tools.

About 35,000 years ago the 'Cro Magnon' race appeared. They were the ancestors of modern humans. This race probably killed off the earlier Neanderthal race.

Homo Erectus making a hand axe.

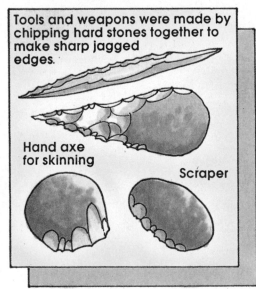
Tools and weapons were made by chipping hard stones together to make sharp jagged edges.

Hand axe for skinning

Scraper

The Cro Magnon race painted beautiful pictures of animals in their caves. Perhaps they believed this would help them when hunting.

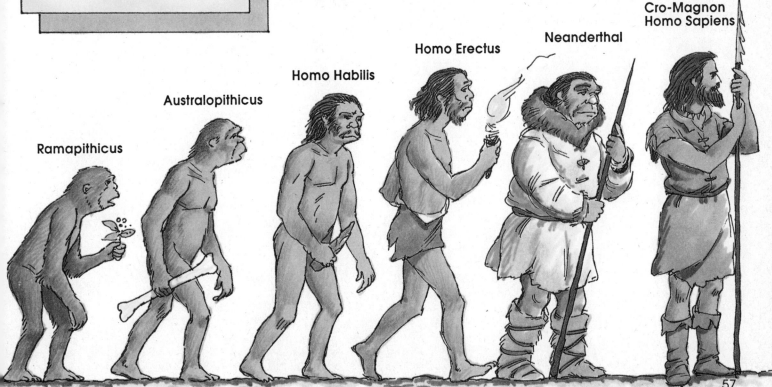

Ramapithicus

Australopithicus

Homo Habilis

Homo Erectus

Neanderthal

Cro-Magnon Homo Sapiens

# Back in time

Early human beings were hunters. To keep warm they wrapped themselves in the fur of the animals they killed. At first they made their homes in caves or they lived in simple shelters made from branches and animal skins.

When early humans learned how to grow crops, and keep cattle and sheep, they had to settle in one place and build a home.

Gradually, people learned to spin wool from their sheep and weave it into cloth. They began to use baskets and pots, and they made tools and ornaments from bronze and iron.

People built their homes in groups to feel safe. A few houses grew into a village, then a town, which in turn became a city.

## The Egyptians

The kings and queens of Egypt were buried in huge stone pyramids built in the desert. These royal tombs held rooms full of treasure, gold, jewellery, clothes and furniture - for use in the 'afterlife'.

The Egyptians wore loose clothes made of linen to keep cool. They used make-up, perfume and wore long wigs and fancy headdresses.

## The Greeks

The Greeks built beautiful temples to their gods. They were great architects and sculptors. They also loved the theatre. Their plays and poems are still read today.

The ancient Greeks began the Olympic Games. This was a sports contest held every four years in Olympia. Chariot races, running, long jumps, discus, javelin, boxing and wrestling were all part of the first Olympic Games.

## The Romans

The Romans were great soldiers. Their armies marched on foot from Italy, into Europe and North Africa. In the lands they conquered they built fine roads, bridges and forts. They founded great cities. You can see the remains of some of their buildings today.

They wore tunics or gowns with a toga on top. The houses of wealthy Romans were very grand, with mosaic floors and pictures painted on the walls. Some houses had under-floor heating, and the public baths had hot pools and steam rooms.

## The Vikings

The Vikings were sea-pirates who raided the coasts of Britain and Europe. They were fierce fighters armed with wooden shields, heavy swords and battle axes. They came from the cold climate of Northern Europe and wore woollen shirts and pants, heavy cloaks and fur-lined leather boots. The women wore bronze and silver brooches on their clothes.

## The Normans

At first the Normans built wooden castles in the middle of a strong stockade.

Later, they built castles of solid stone, often surrounded by a water-filled moat. To enter the castle you had to cross a drawbridge. Some castles were so big they looked like small towns. In times of danger the people would retreat inside the castle walls for safety.

## The Middle Ages

In the Middle Ages all land was owned by a king. A knight gave his services and fought for his king in return for lands and sometimes a castle.

Knights wore chain mail and armour to protect themselves from the swords and arrows of the enemy. Kings, knights and noblemen all had different coats-of-arms or emblems on their flags and shields. They were known by these emblems and could be recognised on the battlefield.

Peasant

Knight

Lady

Nobleman

Jesters were musicians and clowns, their job was to amuse the lords and ladies.

# The Renaissance

This was a time of new thinking and learning. Ideas quickly spread from Italy across Europe because of the invention of printing.

Now people could learn about the latest discoveries in astrology and other sciences.

Explorers sailed away to find new countries and make maps of their voyages. It was also a time for great artists, sculptors and architects.

The scientist Galileo built a telescope to study the stars and planets. He believed, correctly, that the Earth moved and revolved around the Sun, and was not the centre of the universe, as people had thought in the past.

# The Elizabethans

In Queen Elizabeth's reign, costumes were richly embroidered and covered in jewels. Men and women wore starched ruffs round their necks and padding in their clothes.

The Elizabethan seamen were daring adventurers. Sir Francis Drake sailed around the world in the Golden Hind. Sir Walter Raleigh led expeditions of discovery and he named the state of Virginia in America after the Queen. Raleigh also brought the first potatoes back to England.

**William Shakespeare 1564-1616**
He wrote plays and often acted in them in his own theatre, the Globe. His plays have been translated into many languages all over the world.

# The Pilgrim Fathers

Over 100 people left England in 1620 and sailed for America, because they were not allowed to worship as they wanted.

After 66 days at sea in the Mayflower, they stopped ashore at Cape Cod, Massachusetts.

A long hard year followed in which many of them died. In spite of this they harvested their first crops and built new homes. They had so much food they celebrated the first Thanksgiving with their new found Indian friends.

# Georgian Times

In Georgian times fashion became very important. Wealthy people dressed in elegant clothes and cared a lot about the way they looked.

Even children had their own style of clothes and were not dressed like grown-ups, as they had been in the past.

Rich landowners built fine mansions, often taking away the land of the country people. This meant that the villagers had to work for the landowners for a very small wage and often had to leave their homes.

# The Industrial Revolution

This was the age of machines, factories, mills and mines. Spinning and weaving cloth had been done by people in their homes. Now this work could be done much quicker by machines driven by steam engines.

Country people were forced to move into towns and toil in the factories. There, adults and children worked long hours and lived in dirty, crowded slums.

By the end of the 19th century a few caring people worked hard to improve these terrible conditions by passing new laws.

# People around the world

There are around five billion people in the world. All have very different customs and beliefs, speak many different languages and live in very different ways.

Originally everyone belonged to one of three main groups - Caucasoid, Mongoloid and Negroid. Thousands of years ago, the races could not mix. They did not travel from country to country as we do. They were unable to cross great distances, especially over seas, mountains and deserts.

Nowadays it is easy for different races to meet, mix and live together, because travel is quick and easy - especially by air.

**N. American Indian**          **N. American**

### Caucasoid
The Caucasoid people originate in Europe, the Middle East and India. The colour of their skin varies from pale in cool cloudy climates to olive brown in warm climates.

### Mongoloid
This group makes up about 3/4 of the world's population. It includes people who live in South-East and Central Asia, Mongolia, Tibet, American Indians and Eskimos. Their hair is black and straight. They have an extra fold of skin on their upper eyelids.

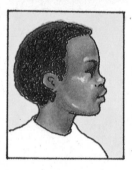

### Negroid
These people have dark brown to black skin. This helps protect them from the rays of the hot Sun, as the Negroid people originate from Africa. Their hair is black and tightly curled.

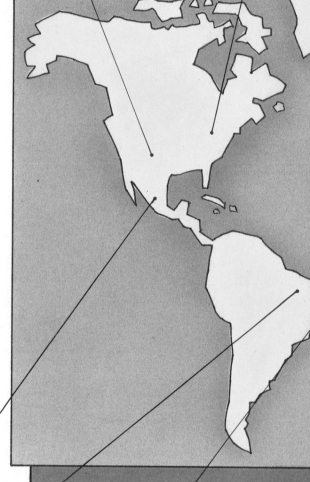

**Mexico**          **Brazil**          **N. Africa**

Eskimo

Britain

Scandanavia

Russia

China

Japan

Africa

Arabia

India

Aborigine

63

# Food

Food contains nutrients that we all need to keep us alive and healthy. It helps us to grow, gives us energy, keeps our bodies warm and helps us to fight infection.

It is important for us to have a well-balanced diet. We should eat a combination of food that contains some proteins, carbohydrates, fats, vitamins and minerals.

## Why food is cooked

When food is cooked, the heat kills harmful germs. Cooked food is easier for us to digest, it also keeps longer and tastes nicer.

**Bake or roast**
Cooking in an oven full of hot air. You can also roast on a spit over flames.

**Grill**
Cooking underneath the heat, or barbecuing over a fire.

**Boil or stew**
Cooking in liquid in a pan.

**Steam**
Cooking in the steam that rises from boiling water.

**Fry**
Cooking in hot oil or fat.

**Microwave**
This special oven cooks food very fast in seconds and minutes instead of hours.

**Proteins**    Help build a strong and healthy body.

**Carbohydrates**    These starchy foods give us energy and warmth.

**Fats**    Our body stores up fat to use as energy and protect us from the cold.

**Vitamins and minerals**    We only need very small amounts of vitamins and minerals every day to keep us healthy.

# How people eat their food

In Europe main meals are eaten with a knife and fork.

In the USA food is cut up first and then eaten with a fork.

Japanese and Chinese food is chopped before cooking and eaten with chopsticks.

In India meals are eaten with the fingers. In the Middle East just the right hand is used.

# Food from around the world

### Sweden
The Swedes eat smorgasbord - open sandwiches that may have smoked or pickled herrings on top.

### Italy
Pizza - with a crisp base and different toppings, and spaghetti - one of the many different shaped pastas.

### Japan
Each dish is beautiful to look at. Sushi is raw fish and rice made into pretty shapes.

### Mexico
Food from Mexico is hot and spicy. Meat and beans are cooked with hot chillies. Tortillas are a thick maize pancake.

### Britain
Roast beef, served with Yorkshire pudding cooked in the meat juices.

### USA
A hamburger and fries, from a fast food take-away restaurant.

### India
Meat and vegetable curries, a lentil dish called daal, and chapatties.

### China
Soup, rice and noodles are served in little bowls. Everyone helps themselves with chopsticks.

### Turkey
Kebabs - meat and vegetables cooked on skewers, with pitta bread that opens into a pocket.

# Your body

The human body is like a super machine, with hundreds of moving parts and miles of tubes. The control centre of the body is the brain.

The brain stores all our learning, controls all that we see, hear and think, and every little movement we make, even while we are sleeping. Here are some of the main parts of your body.

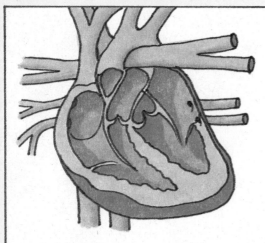

### Your heart
The heart is a muscle that pumps blood around the body every minute of the day. An adult man has 5-6 litres of blood - the heart pumps most of this every minute, but it can pump 20 litres a minute if the man is running fast.

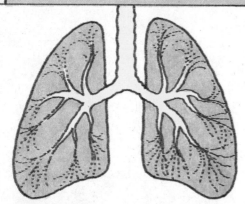

### Your lungs
The lungs are spongy, air-filled organs that take in the air we breathe and supply oxygen to the blood which passes through them. They remove the carbon dioxide from the blood and then breathe it out again. They keep your blood rich in oxygen.

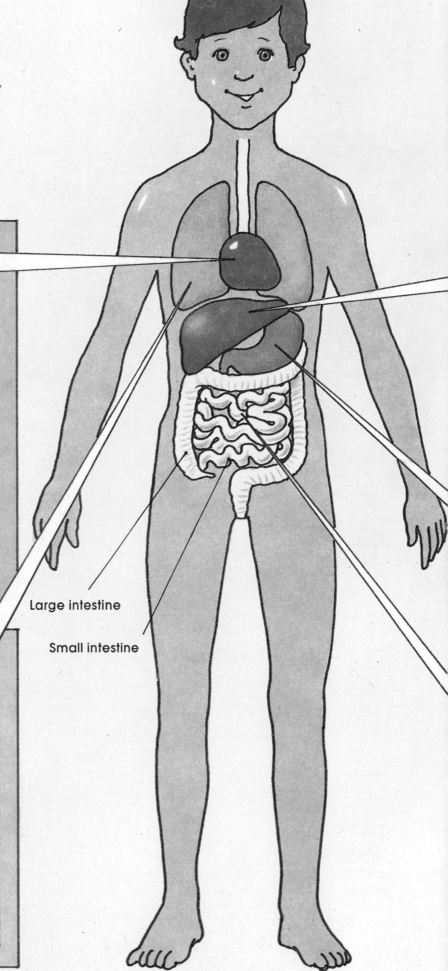

Large intestine

Small intestine

# Your skeleton

The skeleton is the framework of bones that holds us together. There are 206 bones in the adult body. They support our muscles and protect the important organs such as the heart and lungs within the rib cage.

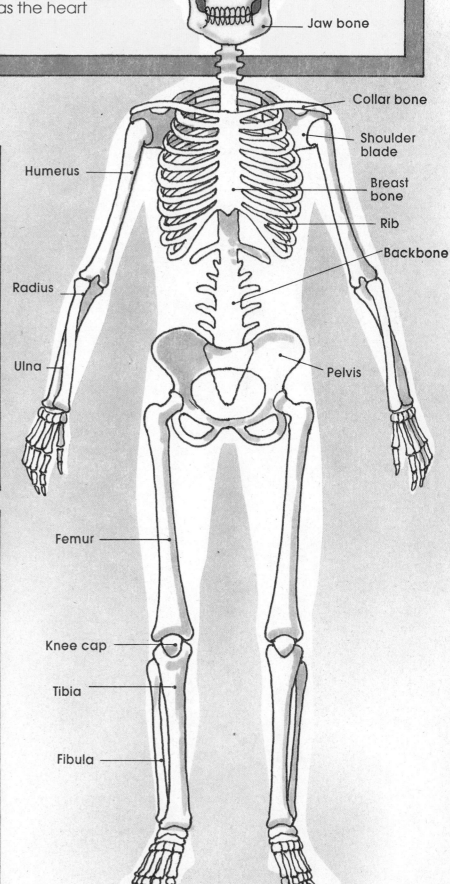

- Skull
- Jaw bone
- Collar bone
- Shoulder blade
- Humerus
- Breast bone
- Rib
- Backbone
- Radius
- Ulna
- Pelvis
- Femur
- Knee cap
- Tibia
- Fibula

## Your liver and kidneys

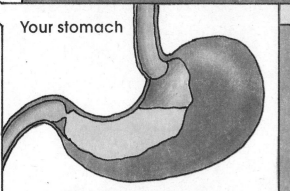

The liver is a very large organ that is vital to our health because it processes and stores the goodness from our food. It also removes old cells from the blood.

The two kidneys, although small, are also vital because they purify our whole bloodstream every hour throughout the day.

## Your stomach

The stomach churns up everything we eat into a soup. Some salts, water and sugar are absorbed into the blood. The soup passes into the small intestine, a 7m (23ft) long tube. Valuable proteins and sugars go to the liver for storage. Unwanted liquids go through the kidneys to the bladder and out of the body. In the large intestine, water is removed and the remaining waste passes out of the body.

# Muscles and joints

If we didn't have muscles we wouldn't be able to move. We need almost 200 muscles to take just one step. There are over 650 muscles in our bodies giving us the strength to lift heavy objects or control the most delicate movements.

The muscles work by pulling (never pushing) on the bones of the skeleton to which they are attached.

Joints are like hinges that join bones together and allow bending, twisting movements. The shoulder and hip joints have the best range of movements.

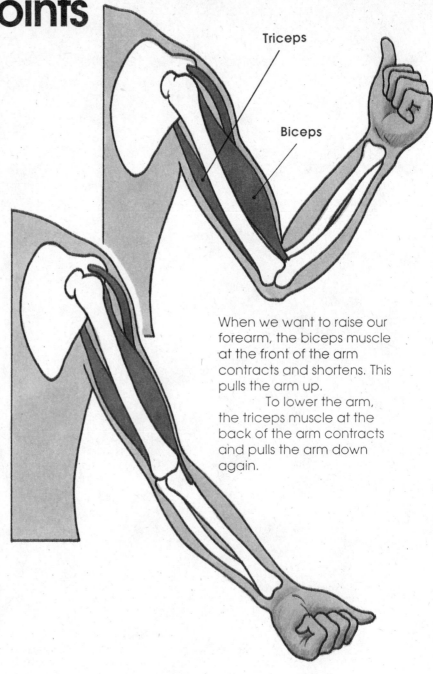

Triceps

Biceps

When we want to raise our forearm, the biceps muscle at the front of the arm contracts and shortens. This pulls the arm up.

To lower the arm, the triceps muscle at the back of the arm contracts and pulls the arm down again.

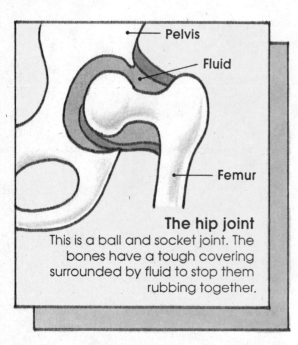

Pelvis

Fluid

Femur

**The hip joint**
This is a ball and socket joint. The bones have a tough covering surrounded by fluid to stop them rubbing together.

---

# Skin, hair and teeth

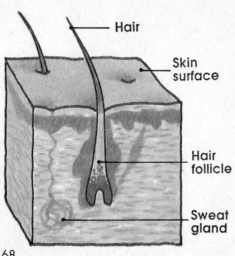

Hair

Skin surface

Hair follicle

Sweat gland

Skin is a waterproof covering over our body. It helps to keep harmful germs out and to regulate our body temperature. When the body is hot the skin sweats and the blood vessels expand.

Hair grows from the skin at about 12mm (1/2 ') a month and each hair lives for about three years, then a new one grows.

Teeth grow from the top and bottom jawbones. We are born without teeth, young children have 20 milk teeth that are slowly replaced around the age of six until we have a full set of 32. These must be kept clean with regular brushing.

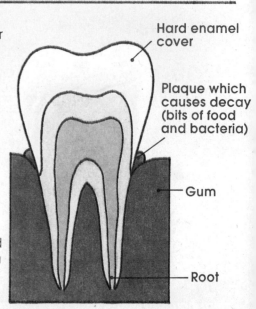

Hard enamel cover

Plaque which causes decay (bits of food and bacteria)

Gum

Root

# The senses

Everyone should have five senses, each one giving us important information. We see with our eyes, hear with our ears, taste with our tongue, smell with our nose and feel through our skin.

## The eye

The human eye is round like a ball. The outer layer is a tough white coat that is clear at the front. Light passes through this, through the pupil and the lens. It then strikes the retina at the back. This tells the brain what it sees.

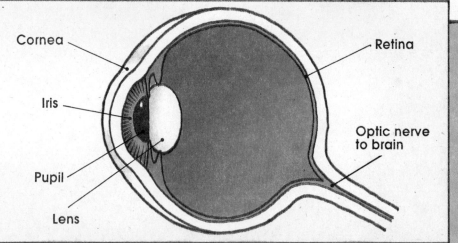

Cornea
Iris
Pupil
Lens
Retina
Optic nerve to brain

## The ear

Sound is a vibration in the air that travels in waves. These waves strike the eardrum, which passes the sound through nerves to the brain, which recognises the sound and tells us what we have heard.

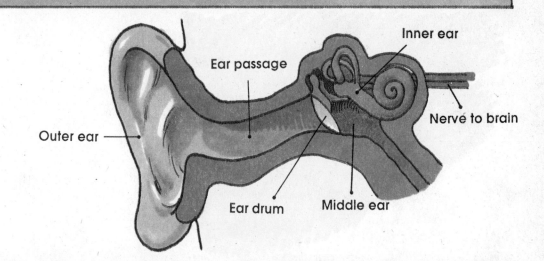

Ear passage
Inner ear
Outer ear
Nerve to brain
Ear drum
Middle ear

## The wonderful brain

The human brain is like a super computer. It stores millions of bits of information that it can recall instantly. We record all the information that our senses gather. This is how we recognise a friend out of all the thousands of people we have seen, or a sound that we have heard maybe years before.

At the same time as it is collecting information from you watching TV or reading a book, the brain is controlling all the thousands of tiny things that are going on in your body - yet this wonderful little creation weighs only about 1.4kg (3lb).

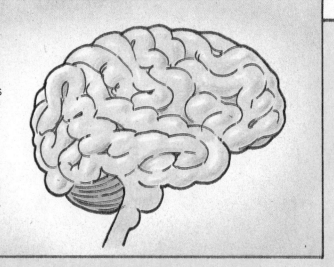

# Transport

When early humans moved from place to place they had to walk. If they needed to move something, they had to carry it. Heavy loads were dragged on sledges, and animals, usually oxen, were used to help. If the load was very heavy it was placed on rollers made from tree trunks. This was a very slow job until, about 5,000 years ago, the wheel was invented.

The first wheel was probably just a slice from a log. This would soon crack and split.

A wheel made of different pieces would be stronger, but very heavy. It was a long time before the spoked wheel was thought of. This meant that wheels could be strong, but lighter.

For hundreds of years people travelled by wagon, and carried trade goods in heavy carts. It must have been very slow and uncomfortable, especially as roads were just muddy, stoney tracks.

The Greeks and Romans used the spoked wheel with a metal rim for their chariots. These were light, fast, two-wheeled carriages. They would often have races.

From the 17th until the 19th century, when the railways came, people travelled long distances by coach. These were drawn by four or six horses that were changed often at special stopping places called stages.

# The steam train

The first public railway in the world opened in 1825. It ran between Stockton and Darlington in England. Thirty-four wagons carrying coal or passengers were pulled by the steam engine (called the 'Locomotion'). This engine was designed by George Stephenson who then built the famous 'Rocket' that ran from Manchester to Liverpool in 1830. He won a prize of £500 for the Rocket in 1829.

Steam transport had begun and soon spread into Europe and America.

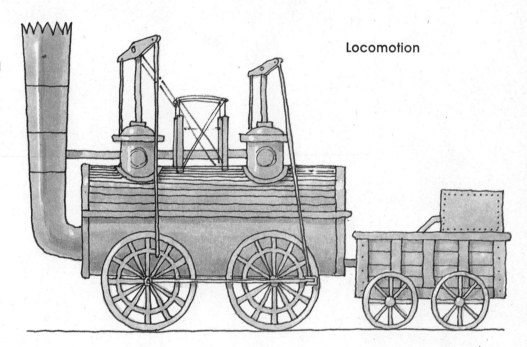

Locomotion

# The motor car

The big change in road transport began when a German engineer, Karl-Friedrich Benz produced the world's first petrol driven motor car in 1885. He then joined forces with Gottlieb Daimler to pioneer the high speed T-stroke petrol engine.

The early cars were called 'horseless carriages' because they still looked like carriages. They were slow and open to the weather, and both driver and passengers wore long coats and goggles for protection.

An early motor car

# Modern trains

From the early days of the Locomotion and Rocket the steam engine grew in speed, size and power. Huge engines pulled trade goods and passengers across continents. In some parts of China, India and Africa these original great steam engines are still hard at work.

The fastest steam train ever was the 'Mallard' or British engine, which reached 201 kph (125mph) in 1938.

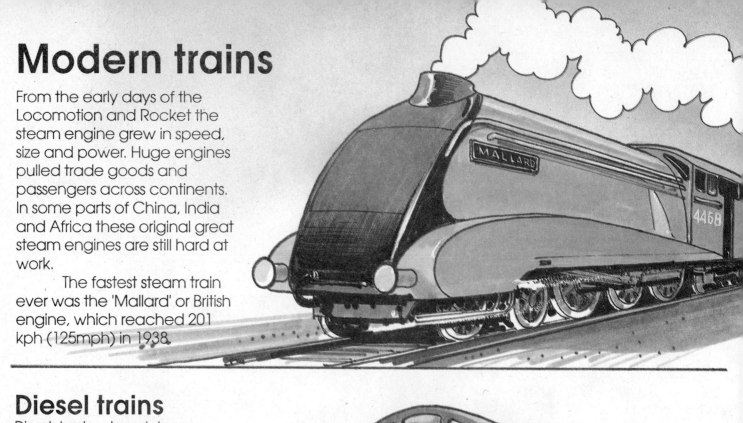

## Diesel trains

Diesels had replaced steam engines by the 1950s. These ran on diesel fuel instead of coal and were therefore much cleaner.

The diesel speed record is 238.9 kph (148.5mph), set in 1987.

## Electric trains

Trains driven by electricity are clean, quiet and fast. A frame called a 'pantograph' on top of the train is in contact with the power cable all the time the train is running.

This French TGV train travels at a speed of 270 kph (168 mph) but can exceed 300 kph (186mph).

# The bullet train

The famous bullet trains have been in service in Japan since 1964. Speeding along at 210 kph (130mph) these trains carry almost half a million passengers a day on the 512km (320 mile) line between Tokyo and Osaka.

# Future trains

Different ideas for the future are being worked on. One that is already working is 'maglev' (magnetic levitation). Magnets make the train hover 15mm (5/8") above a special track. The train has no wheels, no moving parts, and is almost silent when running. In 1987 in Japan, a maglev test train carried passengers at 400 kph (249 mph).

1 Linear motor for forward movement and braking
2 Reaction rail
3 Suspension rails
4 Electromagnets lift the train

# The car

Early cars were very expensive because they were hand-built by craftsmen, using expensive materials.

An American named Henry Ford changed this by building a car that everyone could own. In 1908 he designed the Ford model T and, more importantly, the world's first assembly line to mass produce the car. By 1927 over 15,000,000 of these cars had been sold.

The Ford Model T

# The Engine

The car engine has four or more tubes called cylinders. In each cylinder is a piston that goes up and down and turns the crankshaft that drives the wheels.

1 The piston goes down and sucks in petrol mixed with air
2 The piston goes up again and squeezes the mixture into a small space
3 The spark plug causes an explosion that pushes the piston down
4 The piston goes up and pushes burnt gases out of the cylinders

All of this happens at great speed all the time the engine is running.

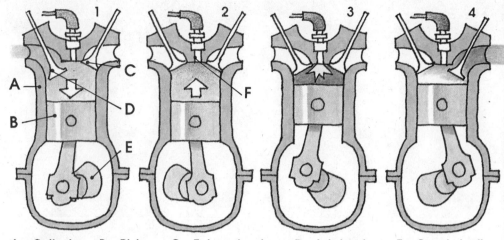

A - Cylinder   B - Piston   C - Exhaust valve   D - Inlet valve   E - Crankshaft
F - Spark plug

This is a sports car, it is very fast to drive.

This is a four-wheel drive vehicle. In most cars the engine drives only two wheels, usually the back. In this vehicle all four wheels are driven - this gives a much better grip on rough or slippery ground.

This is a truck. It carries large amounts of goods to shops and factories. It has a very big powerful engine that runs on diesel fuel, not petrol.

# Bikes

The bike is a very useful machine and great fun.

The first true pedal bicycle was the 'hobby horse' invented in 1839. It was very heavy with iron rims round the wheels.

Modern bikes are made from light alloy tubes and are very strong and fast.

1861- the first front wheel pedalled bike.

Modern BMX bikes are very strong and can be ridden over rough ground.

The motor bike is a high speed two-wheeled machine. It needs skill and training to handle properly.

# Roads and Bridges

The Romans built the first roads. They were long and straight and made of stones set in mortar.

Modern roads are made of concrete surfaced with small stones covered in tar.

Bridge building meant that fast traffic could 'fly over' other roads without stopping. Bridges also carry railway lines over valleys or rivers.

The type of bridge used depends on the span (width) and the weight it has to carry. The Romans discovered the strength of the arched bridge, a design still used today.

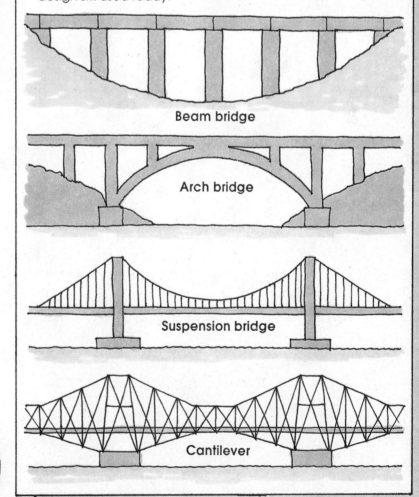

**Beam bridge**

**Arch bridge**

**Suspension bridge**

**Cantilever**

# Ships and boats

Early humans first crossed water by sitting astride logs and paddling across. Later they made rafts by lashing logs together. Then they hollowed out logs to make a canoe.

To make their craft even lighter they stretched animal skins over a wooden frame.

The ancient Egyptians first used ships with a sail on the River Nile about 5,000 years ago. Over the centuries, ships got bigger, with more than one mast and many sails.

**Canoe**
Made from skin stretched over a wooden frame.

**Egyptian boat**
The earliest sail boats. The two large oars at the back were for steering. Similar boats can still be seen on the Nile.

**Greek Galley**
These large, fast ships were rowed by slaves. The point underwater is for ramming.

**Viking Longship**
The Vikings sailed great distances in their shallow bottomed ships, even to North America.

**Arab Dhow**
This ancient craft is still in everyday use in the Middle East.

**Chinese Junk**
Another craft that is still in use after thousands of years.

**The Mayflower**
Some ships have become as famous in history as the men and women who sailed in them. The Mayflower was the little ship that carried the Pilgrim Fathers across the Atlantic ocean to America in 1620. They were seeking the freedom to practise their religion in safety.

## The Clippers

In the mid 1800s there was a great need for fast ships to carry cargo around the world and so the 'clipper' was designed. They were often called 'tea clippers' because they would race from China with a cargo of tea for the merchants of Britain and America.

## Sail and steam

The first steam ships still had sails for extra power. This ship is the 'Great Britain' launched in 1845. It was the first iron-hulled ocean-going ship, and the first propeller ship to cross the Atlantic ocean.

# Why does a ship float?

How can a huge ship made of metal float on water? A ship is hollow so when it is in water it pushes the water out of the way. This principle is called 'displacement', discovered by the ancient Greek, Archimedes.

The weight of the ship pushes down into the water, but the water pushes back with equal force.

Try this at home: take a hollow bowl and put it into water, the bowl will float like a ship. Press the bowl down into the water and the harder you push the more the water will push back to keep the bowl afloat.

# Modern ships and boats

There are many different kinds of ships today, from the giant oil tankers to the little tugs that pull them around. All are designed for a particular job.

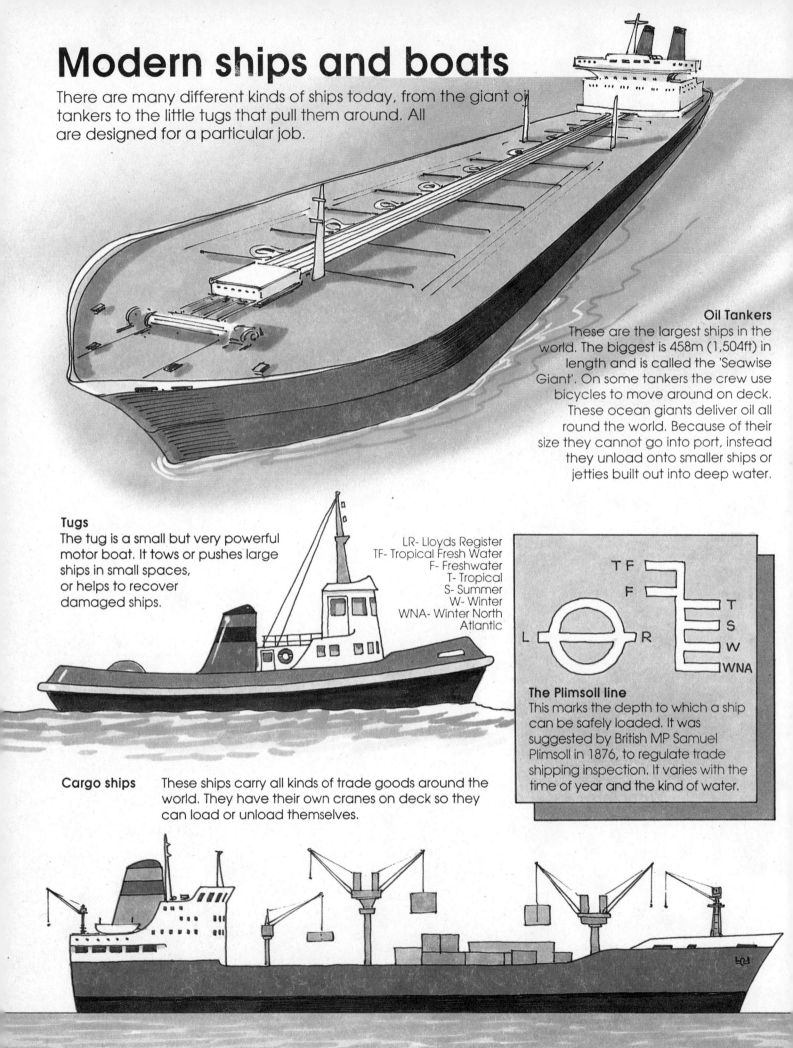

## Oil Tankers

These are the largest ships in the world. The biggest is 458m (1,504ft) in length and is called the 'Seawise Giant'. On some tankers the crew use bicycles to move around on deck. These ocean giants deliver oil all round the world. Because of their size they cannot go into port, instead they unload onto smaller ships or jetties built out into deep water.

## Tugs

The tug is a small but very powerful motor boat. It tows or pushes large ships in small spaces, or helps to recover damaged ships.

LR- Lloyds Register
TF- Tropical Fresh Water
F- Freshwater
T- Tropical
S- Summer
W- Winter
WNA- Winter North Atlantic

## The Plimsoll line

This marks the depth to which a ship can be safely loaded. It was suggested by British MP Samuel Plimsoll in 1876, to regulate trade shipping inspection. It varies with the time of year and the kind of water.

## Cargo ships

These ships carry all kinds of trade goods around the world. They have their own cranes on deck so they can load or unload themselves.

**Hydrofoils**
The hydrofoil looks like an ordinary boat, but below the water it has wings. As it speeds up the wings provide 'lift', just like an aircraft's wings and the boat rises out of the water. This reduces the drag that slows a conventional ship down.

**Fishing boats**
Fishing boats come in all shapes and sizes. The largest are like floating factories, they catch, clean and freeze the fish without having to return to harbour.

**Car ferry**
These amazing ships carry cars, lorries or coaches with all their passengers. The vehicles drive in at one end, and out at the other when they reach their destination.

**Submarines**
These are underwater boats. They have large air tanks down each side. The boat floats when it is full of air and submerges when water is flooded into the air tanks.

# Aircraft

## The first flight

The first flight took place on December 17th 1903 when Wilbur and Orville Wright took off at Kitty Hawk, N. Carolina, USA. Although they only reached a height of 260m (852ft) it proved humans could fly.

## How can a machine fly?

The answer is the engine that pushes the aircraft forward, and the shape of the wing that gives 'lift'.

If you cut through a wing, the shape would be like this picture. The curve on the top of the wing makes the air travel fast over it. This lowers the pressure of the air and the stronger pressure under the wing pushes upwards, giving 'lift'.

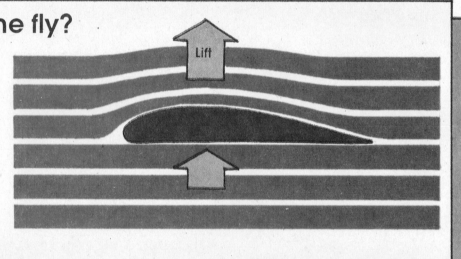

Lift

## The engine

The early aircraft all had 'piston' engines (like a car) which turned a propeller. When a propeller spins it pushes the air backwards very fast, and the aircraft moves forward.

The engine that changed the future of flying was the jet, first invented in 1930 by British engineer Frank Whittle. The jet engine sucks in air that it compresses and heats with burning fuel. The heat and pressure force gases out of the back of the engine at great speed, which pushes the aircraft forward.

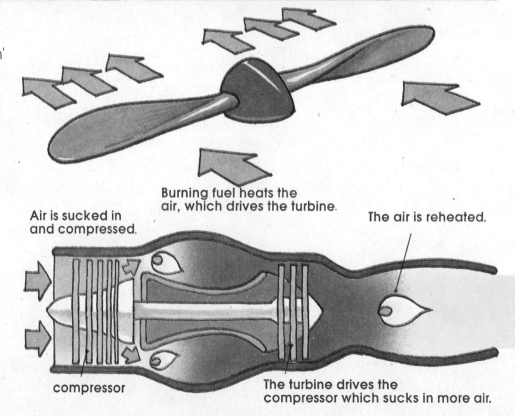

Burning fuel heats the air, which drives the turbine.

The air is reheated.

Air is sucked in and compressed.

compressor

The turbine drives the compressor which sucks in more air.

# How an aircraft manoeuvres

Aircraft have moveable parts on the wings and tail. The pilot uses these to control the movements of the aircraft in the air.

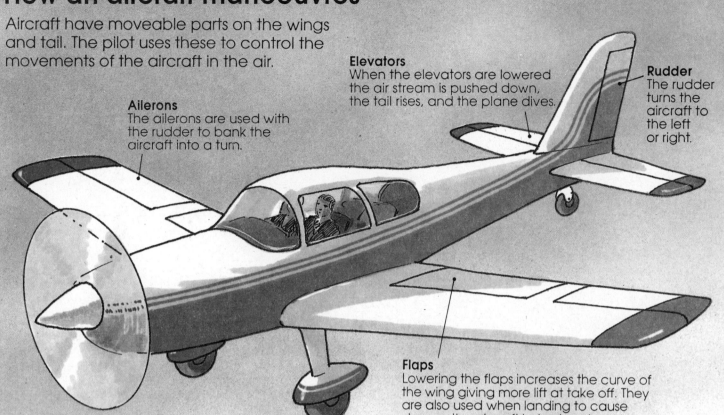

**Elevators**
When the elevators are lowered the air stream is pushed down, the tail rises, and the plane dives.

**Rudder**
The rudder turns the aircraft to the left or right.

**Ailerons**
The ailerons are used with the rudder to bank the aircraft into a turn.

**Flaps**
Lowering the flaps increases the curve of the wing giving more lift at take off. They are also used when landing to cause drag as the aircraft is slowing down.

# Early aircraft

Early aircraft had wooden frames covered with fabric. They needed two or three wings to give lift. As engine wing design improved, the single winged metal plane became possible.

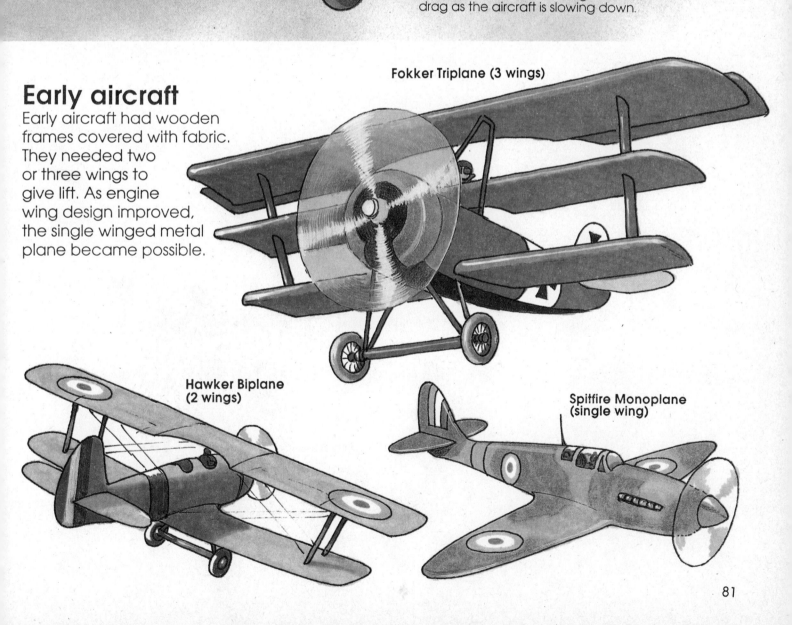

**Fokker Triplane (3 wings)**

**Hawker Biplane (2 wings)**

**Spitfire Monoplane (single wing)**

# Passenger carriers

The powerful jet engine has made it possible for aircraft to carry large numbers of passengers and cargo all around the world in safety and comfort.

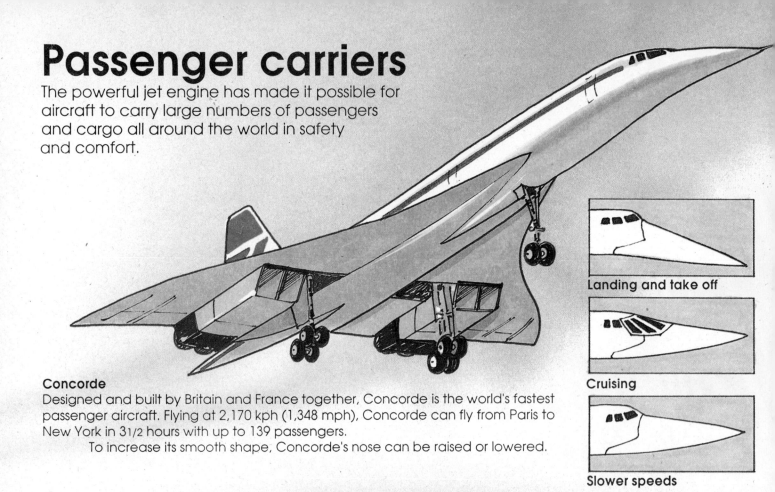

### Landing and take off

### Cruising

### Slower speeds

### Concorde

Designed and built by Britain and France together, Concorde is the world's fastest passenger aircraft. Flying at 2,170 kph (1,348 mph), Concorde can fly from Paris to New York in 3 1/2 hours with up to 139 passengers.

To increase its smooth shape, Concorde's nose can be raised or lowered.

### Boeing 747

Known as the 'Jumbo', this huge aircraft can carry more passengers than any other, over 500.

It has two decks and its four engines give it a top speed of 969 kph (602 mph).

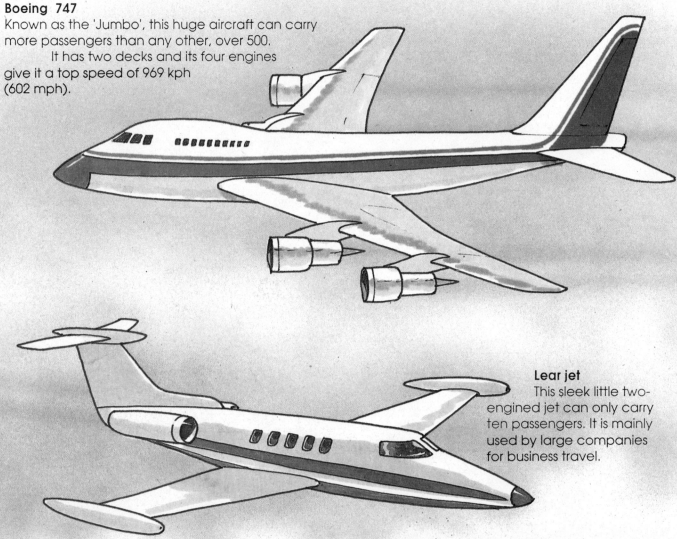

### Lear jet

This sleek little two-engined jet can only carry ten passengers. It is mainly used by large companies for business travel.

# Military aircraft

The search for bigger, faster jet fighters has produced some amazing aircraft.

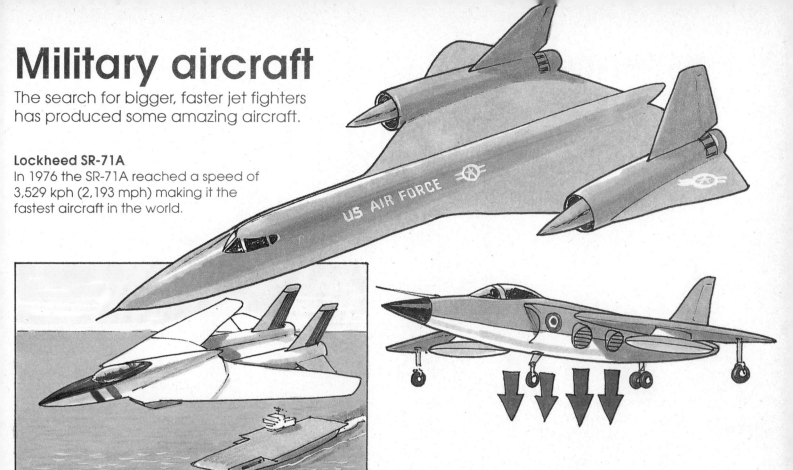

**Lockheed SR-71A**
In 1976 the SR-71A reached a speed of 3,529 kph (2,193 mph) making it the fastest aircraft in the world.

**F14 Tomcat**    This large, heavy jet fighter takes off and returns to an aircraft carrier.

**The Harrier**
This is a vertical take off and landing (VTOL) aircraft. It can thrust its jet engines downwards and then backwards.

# Helicopters

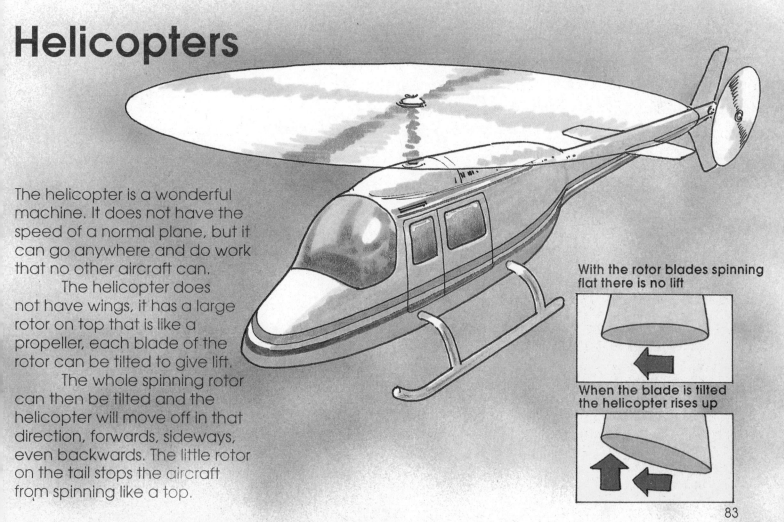

The helicopter is a wonderful machine. It does not have the speed of a normal plane, but it can go anywhere and do work that no other aircraft can.

The helicopter does not have wings, it has a large rotor on top that is like a propeller, each blade of the rotor can be tilted to give lift.

The whole spinning rotor can then be tilted and the helicopter will move off in that direction, forwards, sideways, even backwards. The little rotor on the tail stops the aircraft from spinning like a top.

With the rotor blades spinning flat there is no lift

When the blade is tilted the helicopter rises up

# Communication

Early humans had no written language so we are not really sure how they talked to each other. They may have used signs, or imitated noises made by animals and birds. These simple sounds may have been the beginnings of language.

North American Indians used signs. These mean 'friend' and 'horse'.

## Written Records

From the earliest times, people needed to keep records. About 5,000 years ago, when ancient people wanted to write something down, they drew a simple picture.

### Cuneiform Writing

The Sumerians made wedge-shaped marks in a tablet of soft clay. This was later baked in the Sun.

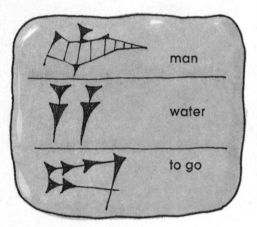

### Hieroglyphics

Priests in ancient Egypt drew simple pictures to represent words. They wrote on papyrus, a paper made from flattened reeds that grew on the banks of the Nile.

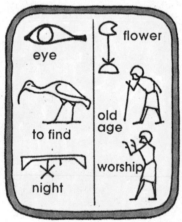

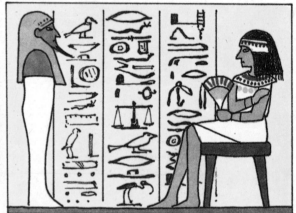

### Alphabets

Later on, letters and symbols instead of pictures were used for each different sound in a word. All these different letters made up an alphabet. Here are some different ones:

АБВГДЕЖ
**Russian letters**

ΑΒΓΔΕΖΗΘΙΚΛΜΝΞ
**Greek letters**

אבגדהוזחטיכלם
**Hebrew letters**

# Books and Printing

As early as the 7th century, the Chinese carved word pictures onto blocks of wood. They spread ink on the raised parts, pressed paper on top, peeled it off and made a print.

Later they cut all their words on separate small blocks so they could move them round to make different sentences. This is called moveable type.

Until the 15th century most books were hand written, then copied by monks or scribes. They were very rare and expensive, but in those days very few people could read or write.

Then in 1450 Johannes Gutenberg set up the first printing press in Germany. It was made from an old wine press, and it used moveable metal type. The first book that he printed was the Bible.

Now books could be made quickly, and this spread new ideas and learning.

Gutenberg's method of printing was called 'letterpress'. He could print 300 sheets a day by hand. Modern printers use a system called 'offset lithography'. Huge machines much bigger than a house can print millions of colour pages a day.

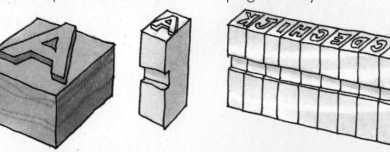

wood letter                    moveable metal type

---

# Sending Messages

Before the invention of the telephone, people had many ways of sending messages: beacon fires, smoke signals, beating drums. Here are some others:

**Morse Code** - a system of dots and dashes for letters. These could be tapped out, or flashed as long or short light signals.

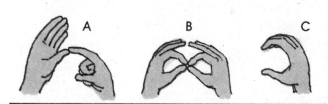

**Semaphore**

The flag positions represent different letters of the alphabet. This method, used by the army and navy, didn't work in fog or darkness.

**Hand spelling** - used by deaf people to make words.

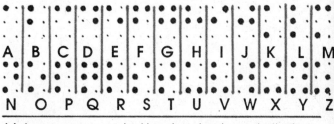

A          B          C

**Braille** - letters made of raised dots that can be felt by blind people.

A B C D E F G H I J K L M
N O P Q R S T U V W X Y Z

Make your own code. Here is a simple code that you can use with friends. Agree with them on a 'keyword' such as 'father' (or any other word). Now write it out, followed by the rest of the alphabet, in order, but without the keyword letters.

F A T H E R B C D G I J K L M N O P Q S U V W X Y Z
A B C D E F G H I J K L M N O P Q R S T U V W X Y Z

Write the full alphabet beneath. To make your words use the top letters instead of the real ones, so 'Hello Paul' would read 'CEJJM NFUJ'.

# Telephones

When Alexander Graham Bell invented a very simple telephone in 1876 he could not have imagined its importance. Today, millions of phone calls are made every day around the world.

When you speak into a phone the sound of your voice is changed into an electrical signal. This signal travels down a wire and is changed back into a voice sound by the phone at the other end. Long distance calls to other countries travel through undersea cables or are bounced off satellites.

**Cordless phone**
This phone is like the normal one except the two parts are not joined by a cord. The 'base' unit is plugged into a wall socket and receives the call, which it sends on to the handset up to 100 metres away.

**Portable phone**
These are radio phones that can be taken almost anywhere. Your phone call travels by radio waves to a nearby transmitter, then through the phone wires to a central computer that passes it on to the person you are calling.

# Answering machines

This is like a tape recorder fitted to your telephone. If you are out, it will answer the phone with a taped message that you have made. It will then record the caller's message for you to play back.

# Telex

Invented in 1916, this office machine sends typed messages through the telephone lines as electrical signals. They are received by a similar machine that types them out again by itself.

# Fax (facsimilie machines)

Fax machines can send copies of printed material around the world in seconds. They work by transmitting the material through a telephone line. The sender's fax machine scans a document or picture, turns it into electrical signals and sends it like a phone call to another machine anywhere in the world. The receiving fax machine is able to interpret these signals and turn them back into a picture.

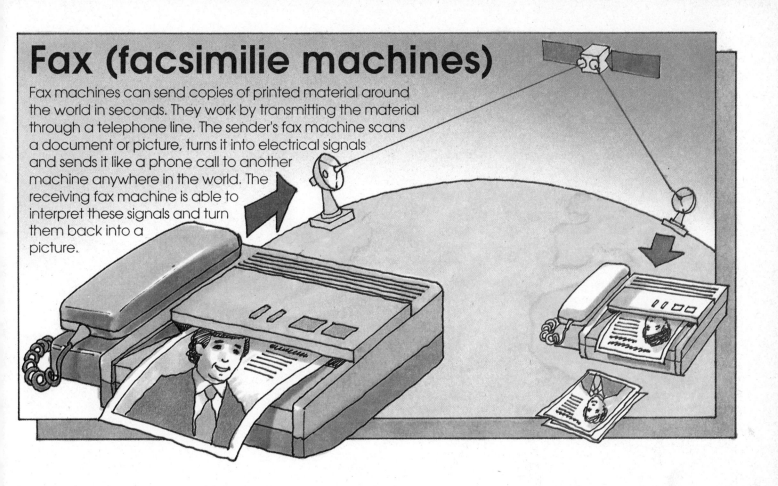

# The computer

The computer is changing our lives faster than anything has ever done before. This machine collects information, sorts it, and stores it in the computer's memory. When you ask it questions, it instantly sorts through the memory and organises all the information in the best way to answer your question in less than a second.

We have been feeding information on every subject into computers for years now. As they can now be linked up to 'talk' to each other, all this information is available in seconds for science, business and education and general use.

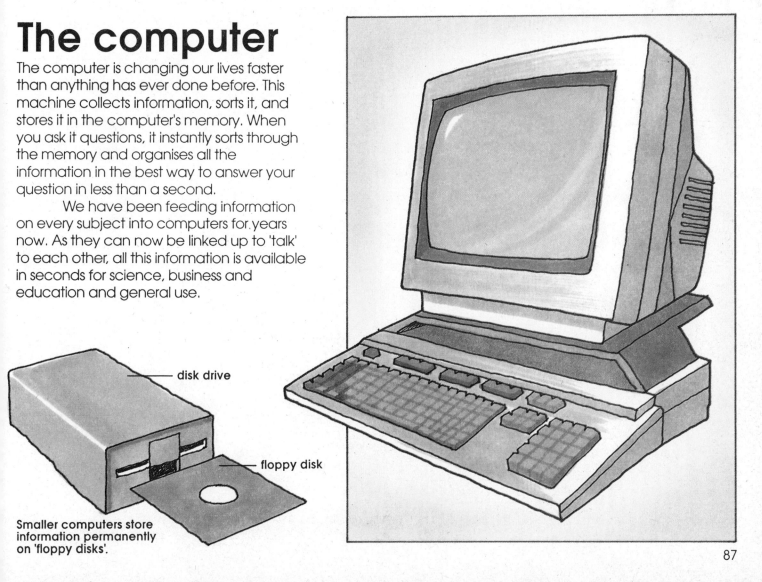

disk drive

floppy disk

Smaller computers store information permanently on 'floppy disks'.

# Television

The first regular TV programmes began in London in 1932. These were all in black and white. Colour TV began in America 20 years later.

Television pictures are made by special cameras that change what they see into electrical signals. These are sent to a transmitter that sends them out to be picked up by TV aerials. They then go into our TV set, which turns them back into pictures, all at the speed of light.

# Satellite TV

The first communication satellite was launched in 1952, meaning that events happening on one side of the world could be broadcast simultaneously on the other side.

Satellite communication works by bouncing signals off a satellite and back to a point over the Earth's surface. Today there are many satellites in orbit.

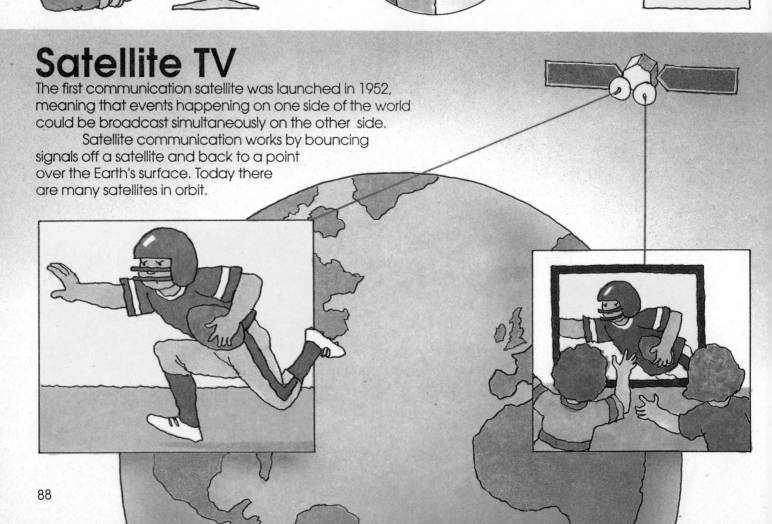

# Radio

The programmes we hear on the radio are carried to us by radio waves. Just like the TV, sounds are changed into signals, and then back into sounds again when they are picked up by our radio aerial.

# Video camera

Video cameras (called 'camcorders') record what they see and hear on a small video tape inside the camera. This can be played back immediately through your TV set, or copied on to a normal video tape.

These cameras are often used by companies to make their own films, or by families sending tapes to distant relatives, in fact, anything that is helped by moving pictures.

# The mail service

When you post a letter it is collected and taken to a sorting office. All the letters are sorted into areas and sent by train to the main town in that area. They are collected in big bags and taken to the post office where they are sorted into streets and roads, then delivered by postmen and women.

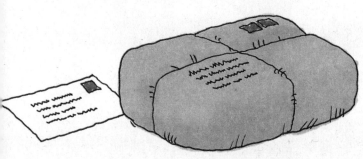

# Books and newspapers

Every day, millions of books and newspapers are printed in many languages. Newspapers tell us what is happening in the world and books record information on different subjects. Libraries lend books to the public. They are divided into fiction and non-fiction books and then classified by subject.

# The journey into space

About 200km (125 miles) above the Earth's surface the atmosphere fades away to nothing and space begins.

There is no air or gravity in space, just a huge emptiness that reaches out to the stars.

The first man-made object to go into space was 'Sputnik 1' launched by the Russians in 1957.

In 1961 they launched the first man into space, Colonel Yuri Gagarin.

For the next few years both Russia and America sent men into space. In 1969, the greatest event happened. America landed two men on the moon, Neil Armstrong and Buzz Aldrin, and brought them safely back to Earth.

**Here are some of the early spacecraft.**

**Sputnik 1**
Weighed only 85kg (187lbs); launched by Russia in 1957.

**Vostok**
The first Russian manned spacecraft 1961.

**Mercury**
The first US manned craft.

**Gemini**
The first two-man craft.

**Apollo**
The first spacecraft to orbit the Moon.

**Soyuz**
Russian spacecraft.

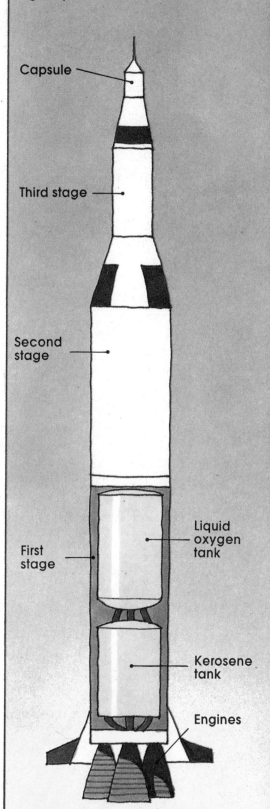

**The Rocket**
To put any craft into space takes enormous power. The American Saturn V rocket has the power of 50 747 Jumbo Jets and travels at 40,000 kph (25,000 mph) to break out of the Earth's gravity.

Capsule

Third stage

Second stage

First stage

Liquid oxygen tank

Kerosene tank

Engines

Burning fuel in the rocket engines creates gases. The gases escaping down and out of the engines create an equal force upwards. This is what lifts the great weight of the rocket.

90

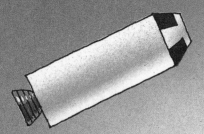

### The three stage rocket
The space rocket is like three rockets one on top of another. All of the fuel in stage one is burned up in minutes so the great weight of the engines and fuel tank can fall away into the sea below. Stages two and three continue the journey to orbit height.

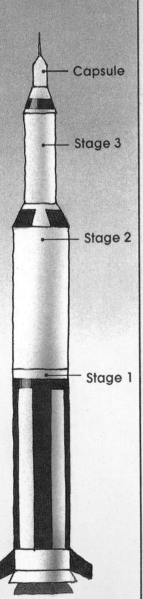

— Capsule

— Stage 3

— Stage 2

— Stage 1

### The space suit
The people who travel in space are called 'astronauts' or 'cosmonauts'.

They must wear special suits when they leave the capsule. The suit has an air supply for breathing; it also protects them from the freezing cold or the direct heat of the Sun.

### Mission badges
These embroidered badges are designed for every new space mission that America launches. The astronauts wear them on their space suits.

91

# Satellites

A satellite is any object that orbits (goes around) a larger object. The Moon is a natural satellite of the Earth.

A large number of man-made satellites now circle the Earth giving us information about the weather, problems on Earth, and help with communications around the world through TV, telephone etc. They also help ships and aircraft to navigate.

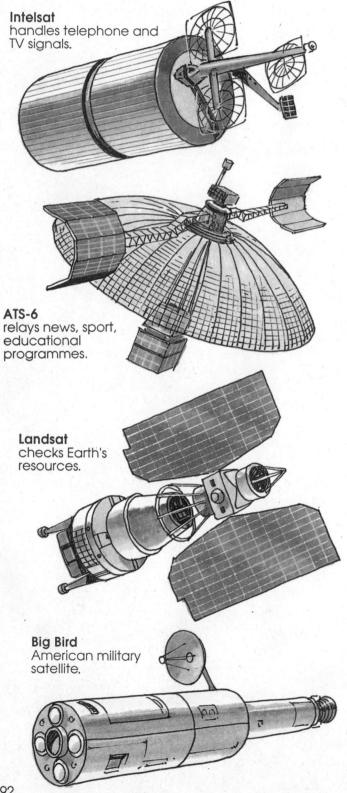

**Intelsat**
handles telephone and TV signals.

**ATS-6**
relays news, sport, educational programmes.

**Landsat**
checks Earth's resources.

**Big Bird**
American military satellite.

# The space shuttle

The American space shuttle is the first spacecraft that is re-useable. It is launched on the back of a huge fuel tank with a rocket on each side.

When the rockets have done their job they drift back to Earth. The giant fuel tank, which cannot be re-used, is allowed to crash.

The shuttle orbits in space to do its work. Most of its body is made up of a big cargo hold with large doors that open for delivery, repairing or recovering satellites. The astronauts go out of these doors to work in space.

When the work is done the shuttle uses its engines to re-enter Earth's atmosphere and then glides back to Earth like a normal aircraft.

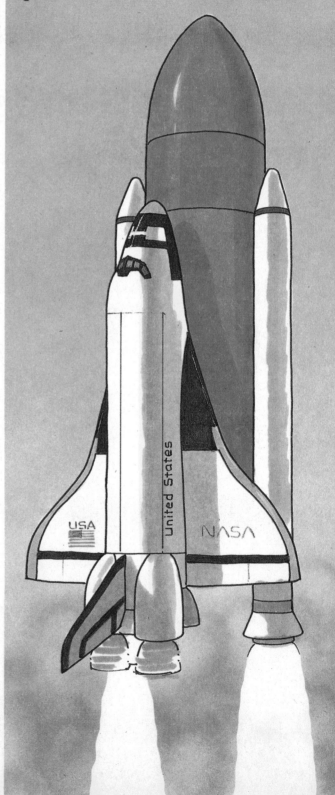

## From launch to landing

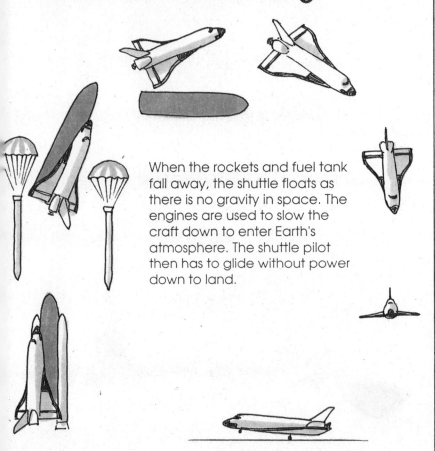

When the rockets and fuel tank fall away, the shuttle floats as there is no gravity in space. The engines are used to slow the craft down to enter Earth's atmosphere. The shuttle pilot then has to glide without power down to land.

## Transporting the shuttle

The shuttle is mounted on the fuel tank along with the rockets inside the 'vehicle assembly building' - one of the largest buildings in the world.

It is then carried to the launch pad on the world's biggest and slowest vehicle, the crawler. It weighs 3,000 tonnes and travels at 1.6kph (1mph) but, amazingly, the driver still has to wear a seat belt.

This picture dictionary is an interesting and
enjoyable way of introducing any young reader to words in everyday use. Words that
need to become part of the modern child's
growing vocabulary.

The use of colourful, fun pictures accompanied by simply constructed sentences will
delight any young learner. At the same time helping them
to recognise, learn and remember a variety of different words.

A humorous and light-hearted approach has been used in both the illustrations and the
text. We hope that this will capture children's
interest and stimulate their desire to read and develop their skills
in writing and spelling.

This is a book to dip into again and again to really learn a lot about words,
or simply have fun.

# THE FUN-TO-LEARN
# PICTURE DICTIONARY

Written by *Anne McKie*. Illustrated by *Ken McKie*.

lamp

Father

cushion

newspaper

television

chair

ceiling

dog

baby

rattle

accident

# Aa

**able**
If you are able to do something - you can do it. I am able to read this dictionary, can you?

**above**
The sky is above the land. Above is opposite to below. The land is below the sky.

**accident**
An accident happens by chance and is always unexpected.

**acrobats**
Acrobats are very good at balancing tricks. You can see them performing on stage or in the circus.

**across**
When you walk across the road, you cross from one side to the other. Take care!

**address**
Your address is where you live. Write clearly when you address an envelope. This helps the postman deliver your letter to the correct address.

MISS JOLLYBEAN
21 THE AVENUE
POPLAR TOWN
MIDSHIRE MD6 2PQ

**adult**
An adult is a grown-up, not a child.

**advertisement**
An advertisement tells you about something for sale. "Ads." are often seen on television, in newspapers and sometimes on the side of a bus.

**aeroplane**
A machine with wings that travels through the air, flown by a pilot. It is often called a "plane".

**afraid**
When you feel afraid, you are frightened.

**after**
1. After can mean later on. Will you wash-up after tea?
2. It can also mean following behind. The fox ran after the goose.

**again**
To do something once more. Do your homework again!

**against**
1. He was standing against the tins. He was next to them.
2. It can mean opposite to. Tom is against washing!

**age**

How many years have you lived? This is your age.

**agree**

To think the same as other people. We all agree your hat is too big.

**ahead**

Ahead means in front of. Go ahead and I'll follow.

**air**

Air is all around. It is a mixture of gases we must breathe to live.

**airport**

The place where aircraft take off and land with cargo and passengers.

**alarm**

An alarm attracts attention. It is often a warning signal.

**alike**

Things that look or are the same.

**alive**

Animals, plants and people are all alive. They are living things.

**all**

All the mice are washing-up. That means every one of them.

**allow**

Allow is to let someone do something. Are you allowed to do that?

**alone**

No one is with me. I'm all alone.

**alphabet**

Here are the twenty-six letters of the alphabet.

ABCDEFGHIJ
KLMNOPQRS
TUVWXYZ

**also**

Also means as well. I have a hamster, also a gold fish.

**aircraft**

The name for different kinds of machines that fly.

*747-Jumbo*

*Helicopter*

*Concorde*

*Fighter*

**always**
The same at all times. The sun always rises in the morning.

**ambulance**
Sick or injured people are rushed to hospital in an ambulance.

**an**
You use this tiny word instead of a, when the word begins with a, e, i, o, u.

an elephant

**and**
And joins words together. Jill and John and Mary are pulling faces.

**angry**
If you are angry you feel very cross about something.

**animal**
Every living creature is an animal.

Monkey
Rhino
Lion
Snake
Humans
Deer
Frog

**annoy**
To make someone cross or tease them. John was beginning to annoy his dad.

**another**
Tell me another story means tell me one more.

**answer**
When we are asked a question, we must give an answer or reply.

**any**
Any can mean some, every or even one. It is often fixed in front of other words.

**anyone**
Is there anyone there?

**anything**
Have you anything to tell me?

**anywhere**
I can't find my glasses anywhere!

**appetite**
When you really want a meal and your dinner smells lovely, it gives you an appetite.

**apron**
An apron tied round you protects you from getting in a mess.

**aquarium**
A glass tank full of water for plants and fish.

**archer**
Someone who shoots arrows from a bow. It is called archery.

**area**
The area is the size of a space or surface.

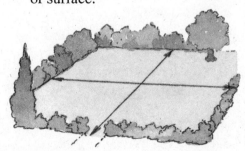

**arithmetic**
Using numbers to add, subtract, multiply and divide.

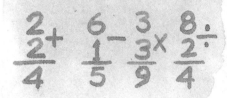

**around**
How would you like to fly around the world?

**arrive**
To reach a place is to arrive. The bus will arrive at ten o'clock.

**artist**
Famous artists produce works of art when they draw and paint.

**ask**
Do you want to know something? Then just ask!

**asleep**
Grandad is asleep in his chair. Soon he will be awake.

**astronaut**
An astronaut is a person who travels in space.

**athlete**
A person who trains hard to be good at sports and games.

**atlas**
A book full of maps.

**attack**
Attack is to begin to fight

**awake**
I can't sleep, I am still wide awake!

**away**
The baby birds have flown away. They are no longer here.

**author**
An author writes books, plays and stories.

**autumn**
The season after summer and before winter when crops are harvested.

# Bb

## baby
A baby is a very young child.

## back
1. Back means behind, opposite to front. Go to the back of the queue!
2. I fell off the stool and hurt my back.

## backwards
When you are on a swing, you swing to the back then move to the front.

## bad
Bad means not good. Uncle is in a bad mood; he has a bad cold.

## badge
Badges are worn by soldiers, scouts and members of clubs. Do you collect badges?

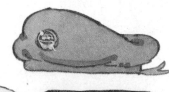

## bag
Bags are containers for holding things and carrying them around.

## bake
To cook food in a hot oven. The baker bakes bread and cakes.

## balance
To hold something or yourself quite steady.

## balloon
Balloons float when blown up, because they are filled with air.

## bank
1. A mound of earth, a river-bank or sand-bank.
2. A building where your money is safely locked away.

## barbecue
Cooking out of doors.

## bare
If you are bare, you have nothing on. If the cupboard is bare, there is nothing in it.

## bark
1. The noise made by a dog. Woof, woof!
2. The rough skin covering a tree.

**barn**
A farm building used for storage.

**barrel**
A large wooden tub to store food and drink.

**base**
The bottom of something. The part on which it stands.

**baseball**
A favourite American team-game like rounders.

**bath**
You can put your whole self in the bath. Remember to wash behind your ears!

**battery**
A battery stores small amounts of electricity. All these things run on batteries.

**beach**
The beach is the strip of sand at the edge of the sea.

**bead**
A little ball with a hole pierced through. You thread beads on a string to make a necklace.

**beak**
A bird's bill or mouth. They all look very different.

**beard**
Hair that grows on a man's face and chin.

**beat**
1. Beat is to hit over and over again.
2. It can also mean to win. I can beat you at tennis!

**beautiful**
Things that are lovely to look at or listen to are beautiful.

**because**
My cousin is angry because a rabbit has eaten all his plants.

**bed**
At night we go to sleep on a bed.

**before**
1. Before means earlier. The tortoise arrived before the hare.
2. It can mean in front of. Who is standing before the drawbridge?

**begin**
To begin with is another way of saying to start with. Begin the book at the beginning!

**believe**
Do you believe in stories about fairies? Do you think they are true?

**bell**
There are many different kinds of bells. They make a ringing noise.

**below**
Below means underneath. A mole digs tunnels below the ground.

**belt**
A thin strip of leather or plastic fastened round your waist.

**bend**
1. A curve in the road is called a bend.
2. A strong man can bend an iron bar.

**beneath**
Another word for lower than. The earth is beneath the sky.

**berry**
Small juicy fruits with seeds. Some are good to eat, some are poisonous.

*Blackberry*

*Strawberry*

*Gooseberry*

*Blackcurrants*

**best**
Susan's cake is best. It is better than all the rest.

**between**
In the middle of two things.

**beyond**
The rainbow is beyond the hills. It is far away, out of reach.

**bicycle**
A bike has two wheels and is pedalled along by the rider.

**big**
An elephant is big, but a whale is bigger. It is the biggest mammal in the world.

*A blue whale can be 20 times heavier than an elephant...*

*and up to 30 metres long*

**billiards**
A game played on a special table with balls and cues.

**binoculars**
A telescope made with two eyes. Binoculars make things seem nearer.

**bird**
All birds have wings and feathers and most of them can fly.

*Goose*

*Owl*     *Robin*

*Heron*

*Ostrich*

*Duck*

*Penguin*

*Cuckoo*

*Swallow*

**birthday**
Your birthday is the day you were born.

**biscuit**
A crunchy flat kind of cake. Yum! Yum!

**bit**
A little piece or fragment of a bigger thing.

**bite**
To bite is to cut into something with your teeth.

**bitter**
Bitter tastes sharp. A lemon is bitter.

**blackboard**
Every school has a blackboard. You write on it with chalk.

**blanket**
A soft warm cover. In winter you snuggle under the blankets.

**blizzard**
A blinding storm with wind and driving snow.

**blood**
The red liquid in your veins. Cut your finger and it will bleed.

**blossom**
A flower is a blossom. Some blossom comes before fruit. Apple, pear and cherry blossom.

**blow**
1. Blow is to make the air move. The wind blows.
2. It can mean a smack or a hard knock.

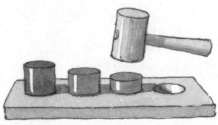

**blush**
When you blush your face turns pink.

**boat**
A boat floats on water. Some have sails and oars, others have engines.

*Rowing boat*

*Sailing boat*

*Speedboat*

**body**
The whole of you is your body.

**boil**
When water is heated it bubbles up and boils. The kettle's boiling!

*Water boils at 100°c*

**bone**
Your skeleton is made up of all the bones inside your body.

**bonfire**
You light a bonfire outside in the garden.

**book**
A book is a collection of sheets of paper bound together. Usually a book contains words and pictures.

**boomerang**
An Australian weapon like a curved stick. When you throw it, it comes back.

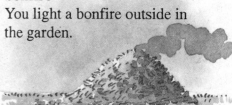

**borrow**
To ask someone for something for a little while. Can I borrow your tie?

**bottle**
A container for holding liquids. You can pour easily from a bottle.

**bottom**
The lowest part of something. The treasure is at the bottom of the sea.

**bounce**
When you bounce you spring up and down again and again.

**bouquet**
A bunch of flowers nicely wrapped.

**bow**
1. There's a bow of ribbon round the box.

2. When you bend over from the waist you bow.

3. Robin Hood shot arrows from a bow.

**bowl**
A hollow, deep dish like a shallow basin.

**boy**
A boy is a young, male child who will grow up to be a man.

**bracelet**
A piece of jewellery worn round your wrist.

**branch**
The branches are the arms of a tree; they spread out from the trunk.

**bread**
Bread is made of flour, water and yeast, left to rise, then baked in the oven.

**break**
1. Break is to smash to pieces.
2. It can also mean a pause. Take a break!

**breath**
Breath is the air you draw in and blow out of your lungs.

**brick**
A block of clay that has been baked, then used to build walls.

**bright**
Ben is sitting in the bright sun in his bright-yellow shorts.

**bring**
Bring is to fetch or carry back. The opposite of take. Bring me my supper!

**broken**
My leg is broken. I must be careful not to break the other one.

**broom**
A long-handled sweeping brush.

**brought**
When the giant shouted for his supper, his wife brought it at once.

**bridge**
A bridge is a way built over a gap so people can cross.

**brush**
A handle with hairs or bristles.
What a lot of brushes we all use!

**bubble**
A transparent ball of liquid,
filled with gas and air, that
floats.

**bucket**
You can fill a bucket with water
and carry it.

**bud**
A flower or leaf before it opens.

**budgerigar**
A cage bird and favourite pet.
You can teach some to speak
very well.

**build**
To build is to make something
by putting several things
together.

**bulb**
1. An electric light bulb lights
up when it is switched on.
2. A flower bulb grows below
the soil and flowers in spring.

**bulldozer**
A big earthmoving tractor with
a blade at the front.

**bump**
When you knock or jolt
something you bump it.

**bungalow**
A house with all the rooms on
one floor.

**bunk**
A bunk is a bed in a ship's
cabin. Have you ever slept in
bunk beds?

**burglar**
Someone who breaks into your
house to steal things.

**burn**
If you set fire to paper it will
burn. Be careful not to burn
your fingers.

**burst**
Prick a balloon with a pin and it
will burst.

**bus**
A bus carries lots of passengers
around. Some buses are double-
deckers. You go upstairs to the
top deck.

**bush**
A small tree or shrub, like a
rose bush.

**butcher**
A man who cuts meat into
pieces to sell for cooking.

**butter**
Cream is churned or whipped
until it thickens into butter.

**buy**
To buy is to pay money for
something. Once you have
bought it, it is yours.

# C c

**cab**
You take a cab in America, a taxi in London. You pay the driver for a ride.

**cactus**
A prickly desert plant.

**cage**
Animals and birds are often kept in a cage. Bars on the sides keep them in.

**cake**
Make a cake, then bake a cake. This is a birthday cake.

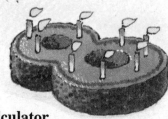

**calculator**
A machine that fits into your pocket. It can add, subtract, divide and multiply.

**calendar**
A calendar shows you the days and dates in each month of the year.

**call**
This word can mean lots of things.
"I am going to call my baby Sophie."
"Call round at my house."
"I must make a phone call."
"Call out if you need me."

**camera**
A machine for taking photographs.

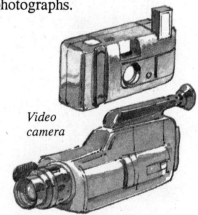

*Video camera*

**camp**
You camp out of doors in a tent on a campsite.

**candle**
A stick of wax with a wick down the middle. The candle burns when you light it.

**cannon**
A very big gun. Some cannons are mounted on wheels.

**canoe**
A light, narrow boat, you sit inside and paddle.

**capital**
1. A large letter of the alphabet.
2. A capital city is the main city of a country.

**captain**
1. The captain is in charge of a ship.
2. The team captain is the leader of the team.

**car**
A motor vehicle with an engine and four wheels used to carry people.

**card**
A stiff piece of paper with lots of uses.

**carpet**
A deep, soft material covering the bare floor.

**carry**
The waiter carried the tray. He took it from one place to another.

**cartoon**
A funny drawing or a short film made with comic characters.

**cassette**
A small flat box that contains the tape for a video or tape recorder.

**castle**
A home for kings and noblemen, with thick, stone towers to keep their enemies out.

**caterpillar**
A grub which becomes a pupa, then turns into a butterfly or moth.

**cattle**
Some cattle are wild like bison and buffalo. Others are domesticated like our cows.

**ceiling**
This is the top of a room, the floor is the bottom.

**cellar**
A room under the house.

**centimetre**
One hundred centimetres equal one metre.

**centre**
The middle of something.

**century**
A century is one hundred years.

**cereal**
Maize, barley, rice, wheat and oats are all cereals.

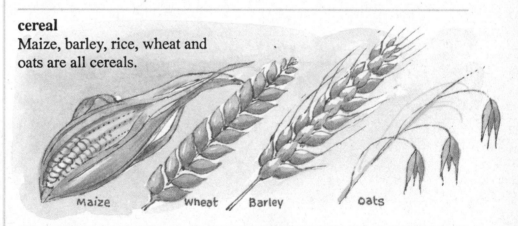

Maize     Wheat     Barley     Oats

**certain**
To be certain is to be sure. I am sure four comes before five!

**chain**
Rings linked together in a row.

**chair**
A seat for one person. Baby Bear had a tiny chair.

**champion**
Champion is another word for winner.

**chance**
1. It happened by chance means just by luck.
2. Give me a chance to win next!

**change**
To make something different. He changed his hairstyle.

**chase**
The goose is chasing the hen, then the duck joins in the chase.

**cheap**
Cheap things cost less money.

**cheer**
To shout and make a noise when your team is winning.

**cheese**
A food made from milk. It has a savoury taste and is good for you.

**chemist**
Someone who makes up medicines.

**chest**
1. A strong box.
2. You puff out your chest when you take a deep breath.

**chief**
Chief means leader. It can also mean the most important.

**child**
A child is a young boy or girl. Fred and Freda are children.

**chimney**
A chimney takes the smoke away from the fire.

**chocolate**
A hot drink or a variety of delicious sweets.

**choir**
A group of singers, often singing hymns in church.

**choose**
Choose is to pick. Can you choose the biggest ice cream?

**chop**
Chop means to cut into pieces or to cut down.

**Christmas**
This is the time that people celebrate the birth of Jesus.

**church**
People pray and worship in a building called a church.

**cinema**
A large building where films are shown to the public.

**circle**
A perfectly round figure like a ring.

**circumference**
The distance round a circle.

**circus**
A travelling show with clowns, animals and acrobats.

**city**
A very large town is called a city.

**clap**
To strike your hands together. When an audience claps it is called applause.

**class**
A group of people learning things together.

**classroom**
A room where the class meets for lessons.

**clay**
Wet, soft, sticky earth that is made into pots or bricks and baked hard.

**clean**
Clean is well washed and not dirty at all.

## cliff

A cliff is a steep rockface. Do not go near the edge!

## climate

The different kinds of weather in all sorts of places.

## clock

An instrument that measures and tells us the time.

## close

1. Close means to shut. Close that window, I'm in a draught!

2. It can also mean near. Sit close by me, I feel lonely!

## clothes

All sorts of different things to wear made of cloth.

## cloud

A cloud is made up of tiny drops of water floating together in the sky.

## clumsy

A clumsy person is awkward, and bumps into things.

## coach

1. A coach is a teacher or trainer.
2. It is also a bus or a railway carriage.

## coal

A hard, black rock dug out of the ground. It makes a lovely fire.

## cobweb

A spider spins a silken cobweb to trap insects.

## coconut

A huge, hairy nut that grows high up in a palm tree.

## coffee

Coffee beans are roasted and ground up. Add boiling water and you have a lovely cup of coffee.

## coin

A piece of money made of metal.

## cold

It is always cold in winter. Now is the time you catch a cold.

## collar

A shirt collar fits round your neck. The dog has a collar round his neck too.

## coast

Where the land meets the sea.

**collect**
Collect means to gather together.

**colour**
There are many colours, here are just a few.

**come**
To come means to move near and not go away.

**comma**
A comma is a punctuation mark. It divides two parts of a sentence.

**compare**
You notice if things are alike or different, you compare them.

**compass**
You can find your way if you have a compass. The needle always points north.

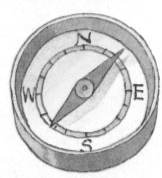

**complete**
Complete has nothing missing. This puzzle is complete.

**computer**
A machine that can store, process and give out large amounts of information at very great speed.

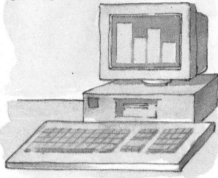

**concert**
A musical entertainment given by an orchestra, a band and sometimes a choir.

**cone**
A cone is round and flat at the bottom and goes to a point at the top.

**conjuror**
A conjuror does magic tricks.

**connect**
Connect means to join together.

**construct**
Construct is to make or build. Boys love construction toys.

**continent**
A large mass of land. The Earth is made up of seas and continents.

**cook**
A person that makes a meal ready to eat. I cooked the breakfast this morning!

**cool**
Cool feels a little bit warmer than cold. On a hot day the water feels cool.

**copy**
To make something that is exactly like another.

**corner**
A street corner is where two streets meet. Two straight lines meeting make a corner.

**correct**
Right, with no mistakes at all.

**cosmonaut**
A Russian spaceman.

**costume**
Putting on a costume means dressing up. In some countries national costume is worn.

Mexico

Japan

Lapland

**cottage**
A little house in the country.
Here is a thatched cottage.

**count**
To count is to add up how many there are.

**country**
1. When you leave the town and begin to see fields you are in the country.
2. A country is a land and all its people, America; Spain; China.

**cover**
"Cover me up in bed. I have such a pretty, blue cover."

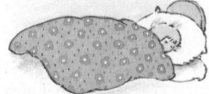

**cowboy**
A man in charge of herds of cattle on a ranch.

**crab**
A crab is a sea creature with a hard shell and two claws like pincers.

**crack**
1. A sharp noise like the crack of thunder.
2. A very fine split. This cup is cracked!

**cradle**
A bed for a baby.

**crash**
1. A sudden fall which makes a loud noise.
2. An accident when people or things are smashed.

**crawl**
To move around on your hands and knees.

**crayon**
A coloured, wax stick for drawing pictures.

**creature**
All living things except plants.

**crime**
A wrong deed. This burglar has committed a crime.

**cross**
1. These lines are in the shape of a cross.
2. When we are cross we feel angry.
3. Cross the road with care.

**crowd**
Many people all together in one place.

**crown**
The head-dress of kings and queens, made of gold and jewels.

**cry**
1. When you cry, tears fall from your eyes.
2. When you cry for help, you shout loudly.

**cube**
A solid shape with six equal square sides.

**curtain**
Cloths that cover windows or make a screen on the front of a stage.

**curve**
A bent line that has no straight part.

**cushion**
A soft, fat pillow usually on a chair.

**customer**
A person who goes into a shop to buy something.

**cut**
To divide into pieces with scissors, a knife or a saw.

**cycle**
Another word for bicycle. I cycled through a puddle.

**cylinder**
A shape like a tube. It can be solid or hollow.

# D d

**daily**
Daily is every day. The newspaper is delivered daily.

**dairy**
Milk is kept at the dairy. Often cheese, butter and yoghurt are made there.

**damage**
The storm caused a lot of damage, it did a lot of harm.

**damp**
Damp means slightly wet. Babies are sometimes damp!

**dance**
Dance is to move around to music. The waltz is a dance.

**danger**
Danger is something harmful. How very dangerous!

**dark**
Dark means no light. Witches go out on dark nights, dressed in dark clothes.

**date**
The date tells you the day, the month and the year.

**daughter**
The female child of her parents.

**day**
A day lasts twenty four hours. There are seven days in a week.

**decide**
If you make up your mind, you decide.

**deck**
The deck is the floor of a ship.

**decorate**
When you decorate a room for a party, you make it look pretty.

**deep**
Deep goes a long way down. In Switzerland the snow can be very deep.

**delicatessen**
A shop selling cooked meats and cheeses from different countries.

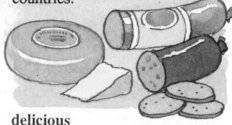

**delicious**
Something good to eat tastes delicious.

**deliver**
When the postman delivers the letters, he hands them over to you.

**dentist**
The dentist takes care of your teeth.

**describe**
To write or tell someone about something.

**desert**
A land where there is very little water and nothing can grow.

**desk**
A little table which sometimes has a sloping top. You sit at a desk to write and read.

**detective**
A person who tries to solve a crime.

**detergent**
We use all kinds of detergents when we are spring cleaning. They help dissolve the dirt.

**diagram**
A drawing or plan that helps explain things.

**diamond**
A very hard precious stone. It has to be cut and polished before it is made into jewellery.

**diary**
A daily record of events. You make notes in your diary as a reminder.

**dictionary**
A book that tells you the meaning of words.

**different**
Different means not the same. Can you spot the difference?

**difficult**
A difficult thing is hard to do, not easy.

**dig**
You dig the earth with a spade. A machine called a digger can dig deeper and faster.

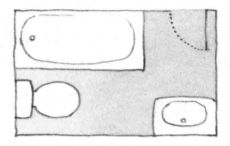

**dinosaur**
These great reptiles lived on Earth millions of years ago. Now they are all gone.

**direction**
The way in which you go. You're going in the wrong direction!

**dirty**
If you need a wash, you are dirty.

**disappear**
If something has disappeared, it has vanished and can't be found.

**discover**
This means to find something. Christopher Columbus discovered America.

**disguise**
A disguise changes the look of something or somebody!

**dish**
A dish is a shallow bowl or plate like a pie dish.

**distance**
Distance is the space between two things or places.

**dive**
To jump or fall head first into something. You dive into the water and you make a dive for the ball.

**do**
Do is to carry out a thing. Busy people are doing things all day long!

**doctor**
A doctor looks after people who are ill.

## dolphin

Dolphins are intelligent and playful creatures. They swim very fast in groups, then suddenly leap out of the water high into the air.

## dome

A dome has a shape like half an orange. A dome is usually placed on top of a building.

## door

To enter a room or building you have to go in by the door.

## double

1. Double is twice as much.
2. Do you have a double? Someone who looks just like you.

## down

Down means to go lower down from that ladder!

## dragon

Dragons can be found in fairy tales and legends.

## draw

You use a pencil, a crayon or chalks to draw. Who drew that?

## drawer

An open box that slides in and out of some pieces of furniture.

## dream

The thoughts that come into your head when you are asleep.

## drink

To drink is to swallow a liquid. What would you like to drink?

## drive

1. To drive is to make any vehicle travel along.
2. When the farmer drives his geese into the pens, he makes them go inside.

3. The drive is the road leading up to a house.

## drop

1. Drop is to let something fall.
2. It also means a little blob of liquid.

## drown

If you sink below the waves and breathe in water instead of air, you drown.

## dry

Dry has no wet at all. Rub the baby dry, then hang the towel out to dry!

## during

During the storm I hid under the bed. During means while it lasted.

## dye

If you dye a garment or your hair, you change the colour by using different dyes that stain.

# E e

## each
Each means every one. Each dog has a spot!

## eager
If you are eager, you are very keen to do something.

## ear
People and animals hear with their ears.

## early
Be in good time, be early!

## earth
1. We live on a planet called Earth.

2. Earth is another name for soil.

## earthquake
When the ground trembles and cracks open.

## easel
A stand for a painting or a blackboard.

## east
The sun rises in the east. China and Japan are to the east of the map.

## easy
Easy things are simple to understand or do. Never hard or difficult.

## eat
When you eat you put food into your mouth, chew it, then swallow. Have you eaten your semolina?

## echo
A sound which bounces back again and again from the walls of mountains or caves.

## edge
The end or side of something. Don't fall off the edge!

## egg
All birds and a few animals live inside eggs before they hatch.

## either
Either means one or the other of two things. You can have either a cake or a carrot.

## electricity

Electricity is power that reaches us along wires. Many machines run on electric power.

## emergency

When something very unexpected happens and must be dealt with.

## empty

Empty has nothing in it. My bag was full but now it's empty!

## encyclopaedia

A book or several books that contain information on most subjects.

## end

The last part or finish of something. This is the end!

## engine

The engine makes the power that drives the machine.

## enormous

Enormous is very, very big. Do giants have enormous feet?

## enough

As much as you need and no more. Have you had enough?

## enter

When you enter you go in. You can enter a room. You can also enter a competition.

## envelope

A folded paper cover usually for a letter.

## equal

Things that are equal are the same in size and value.

## equator

The imaginary line round the centre of the Earth.

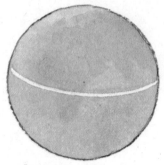

## escalator

A moving staircase often in a store or hotel.

## escape

To get away, be free. My beetles have escaped!

**even**

1. An even number can be divided by two.
2. An even surface is flat and smooth.

**evening**

The end of the day when the sun sets, before night.

**ever**

Ever means always. I will love you for ever!

**every**

Every means each one. We get older every minute.

**everybody**

Everybody means all people. Everybody is born!

**everything**

Everything means all things. Everything in the room was yellow.

**everywhere**

Here, there, everywhere; dust gets in all places.

**exactly**

This piece fits exactly. It is just right.

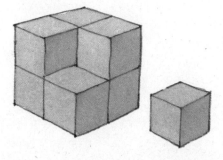

**excellent**

Excellent means very, very good. Your exam results are excellent!

**excited**

To be thrilled with pleasure about something. I am very excited about this trip!

**exercise**

1. Exercising your body keeps you fit.

2. Doing exercises on the flute helps you to play better.

**exit.**

The way out.

**explain**

"Can you tell me why you are such a mess?" Then you have to explain.

**explode**

When something bursts or blows up it explodes with a loud bang.

**explore**

To examine a thing you have not seen before. An explorer finds new places and countries.

**extinct**

Something that has died out is extinct. The dodo is extinct.

**extra**

Extra means more than you have. I would like extra gravy on my meat!

**eye**

You have two eyes. They are used for seeing. If you have good eyesight, you are able to see well. If you lose your sight and cannot see, you are blind.

# F f

**fable**
A fable is a short story with a moral. Aesop wrote many famous fables.

**face**
At the front of your head under your hair is your face.

**fact**
A fact is something that can be proved to be true.

**fail**
To fail is to try but not manage to do something.

**fairy**
A tiny creature that is believed to be magic. Do you believe in fairies?

**fall**
Fall means to drop down. An apple has fallen on my head!

**false**
False means untrue or not real. Is he wearing a false nose?

**family**
Your family are people related to you.

**far**
Far is a long way off. The ship sailed far away.

**farm**
A farm is the land and buildings where crops are grown and animals kept.

**farmer**
The person who lives and works on the farm.

**fast**
Fast is very quick. A speedboat is faster than a rowing boat.

**fasten**
You must fasten your safety belt. If it is closed you will be safe.

**father**
A father is the male parent of his children.

**favourite**
Favourite things are the things you like best.

**fear**
To fear is to feel you are in danger. Are you afraid of the dark?

**feather**
Feathers cover a bird's body. The large feathers help it to fly and the down helps the bird to keep warm.

**feed**
To feed is to give someone food. A robin feeding her young.

**feel**
To feel something is to handle it and touch it.

**fence**
If you enclose your garden, you put up a fence as a barrier.

**fern**
A plant with feathery leaves. Ferns love cool shady places.

**few**
If you have a few sweets, there are not very many.

**field**
A piece of land for growing crops or grazing animals.

**fierce**
Some wild animals are savage and frightening. They are very fierce.

**fight**
When you fight you argue with someone and often hit them.

**figure**
A figure is the shape of a number or a person.

**fill**
To leave no space for any more.

**film**
1. A film is a moving picture at the cinema or on television.
2. You take photographs on a film inside a camera.

**find**
To discover something that was lost, or that you didn't know was there.

**fine**
1. A fine day is always warm and sunny.
2. A hair is fine. It is thin like a thread.

**finger**
Fingers are at the end of your hands. You have eight fingers and two thumbs.

**fire**
If something is on fire it is burning. Send for the fire brigade! A fire engine will come as soon as possible with firemen on board. When the blaze is put out they will return to the fire station.

**firework**
You must treat fireworks with care because they explode. We all love fireworks on Bonfire Night.

**fish**
A fish is a swimming animal which lives in the water. They can breathe underwater through their gills.

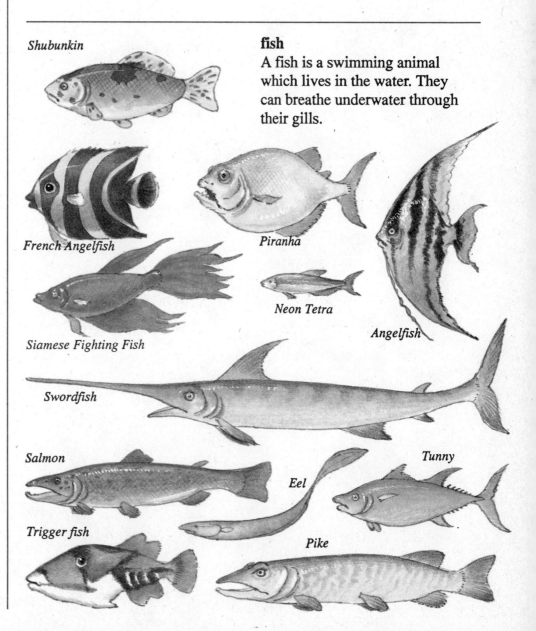

*Shubunkin*

*French Angelfish*

*Siamese Fighting Fish*

*Piranha*

*Neon Tetra*

*Angelfish*

*Swordfish*

*Salmon*

*Eel*

*Tunny*

*Trigger fish*

*Pike*

**fit**
1. Keep fit, stay healthy.
2. If your shoes do not fit, they are either too big or too small.

**flag**
A piece of cloth with an emblem on it. Each country has a flag of its own.

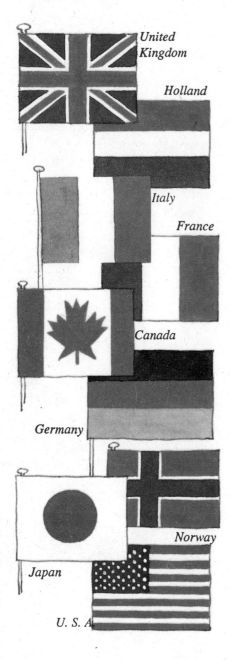

United Kingdom

Holland

Italy

France

Canada

Germany

Japan

Norway

U. S. A.

**floor**
You walk on the floor. It is the lowest part of the room.

**flour**
Flour is the soft, white powder made from crushed grains of wheat.

**flower**
Flowers are made up of brightly coloured petals, inside which are the seeds.

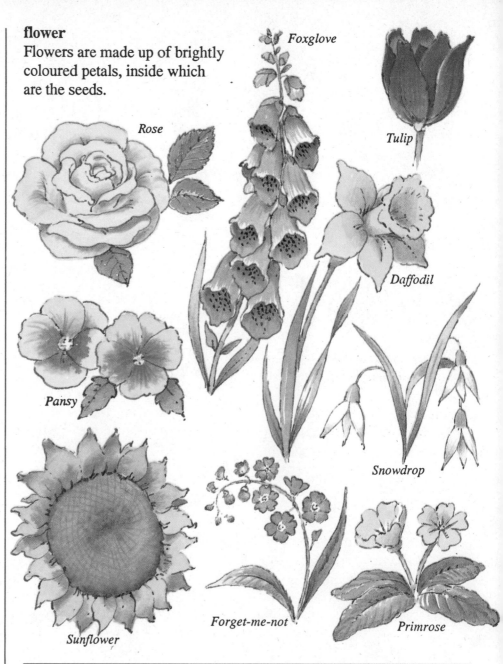

Foxglove

Rose

Tulip

Daffodil

Pansy

Snowdrop

Sunflower

Forget-me-not

Primrose

**fly**
1. If you move through the air you fly. Many things fly all by themselves.
2. There is a tiny insect called a fly.

**follow**
"Follow me," said the fox, "I will lead and you can walk behind."

**food**
To stay alive we must eat food.

**foot**
The lowest part of your leg from your ankle to your toe is your foot.

**forest**
Lots of trees growing together in one big area.

**forget**
If you don't remember things, you forget them. Have you forgotten the time?

**free**
1. If a thing is free it costs nothing at all.
2. Prisoners are not free, they cannot come and go as they please.

**freeze**
When water freezes it gets very cold then turns to ice.

**fresh**
Fresh means new and clean. Food that is fresh has just been made or picked.

**friend**
A friend is someone you know very well and like a lot.

**fright**
What gives you a fright or scares you?

**front**
Front is the part that faces forward. A man in the front seat of his car is parked in front of the house.

**fruit**
The seeds of a plant grow inside the fruit.

Apple

Pear

Banana

Peach

Strawberry

Cherries

Blackberry

Gooseberry

Lemon

Melon

Hazelnut

Brazil nut

Orange

**fry**
When you fry food you cook it in hot fat or oil.

**fun**
You laugh when you are having fun. Cartoons are funny.

**fur**
The hair that covers an animal's body is called fur. What a furry creature!

**furniture**
Houses are full of furniture. We use these items every day.

# Gg

### gain
To gain is to increase. It is the opposite of lose. I have gained weight.

### gale
When there is a gale blowing, the wind is very strong indeed.

### gallery
You go to a gallery to see works of art.

### game
In any game you play, you must keep to the rules.

### garage
A place where cars are kept or repaired.

### garden
A garden is a space, usually round a house, for growing flowers and vegetables. You can relax and play in your garden.

### gate
A gate is an outside door in a wall, hedge or fence.

### geese
A flock of geese is a lot of geese together. One bird on its own is a goose.

### gentle
A gentle person is loving and careful, not rough in any way.

### geography
In geography we learn all about the Earth, the animals, the people and the way they all live.

### germ
Germs are so tiny you can only see them under a microscope. They can cause disease.

### giant
A thing or person that is huge. There are lots of giants in fairy tales.

### gift
A gift is a present, something that is given.

**girl**
When your mother was young she was a girl. A girl grows up to be a woman.

**give**
If you give a thing away you do not ask for it back.

**glad**
I am glad you came, means I am very happy that you came.

**glass**
You can see right through glass. Although it is very hard, it breaks easily.

**globe**
The globe is shaped like a ball and has a map of the world on its surface.

**glove**
Gloves cover your hands and keep them warm. They have a separate little cover for each finger.

**glue**
You can stick things together with glue. It is often very sticky.

**go**
Go means to leave one place for another. You go your way, I'll go mine.

**goal**
To score a goal is the purpose of some games.

**gold**
Gold is a very precious yellow metal.

**goggles**
They fit tightly to your face and protect your eyes, you can still see properly.

**good**
1. He is a good boy, he is well behaved, not naughty.
2. Her work is very good. It is first class!

**goodbye**
You say goodbye when you are parting from someone.

**govern**
To govern is to rule and guide people. A government is a group of people who promise to do this.

**grab**
When you grab something you catch hold of it suddenly. I grabbed a bun before mother grabbed me!

**grandfather**
My father's father and my mother's father are my grandfathers.

**grandmother**
My father's mother and my mother's mother are my grandmothers.

**grass**
Grass is green with thin sword-shaped leaves.

**great**
1. Abraham Lincoln was a great man. He was an important man. He became President of the United States of America.

2. A great shadow fell across the path. It was a very big shadow.

**greedy**
A greedy person always wants more for himself.

**greenhouse**
A building made of glass where plants are grown.

**grin**
A great big smile!

**ground**
Everyone walks on the ground. It is the Earth's surface.

**grow**
To grow is to get bigger. My how you've grown!

**guard**
The soldiers are on guard looking after the Queen and keeping her safe.

**guess**
To say or think something you don't really know.

**guide**
To guide is to show the way. Guide-dogs lead blind people.

**gun**
A dangerous weapon that fires bullets. Cowboys carry guns.

**gymnasium**
A large room where people keep fit on special apparatus.

# H h

**hair**
Hair grows on the bodies of animals and humans. Some people are more hairy than others.

**half**
If you cut something in half you get two pieces of equal size. Each one is called a half.

**Hallowe'en**
The thirty-first of October is Hallowe'en, the night that witches fly about.

**halt**
When you are told to halt, you must stop moving at once!

**hamburger**
A round, flat cake of minced beef, often served in a bread bun.

**handle**
A hammer has a handle. Be careful how you handle it!

**handwriting**
The way you write with a pen or pencil.

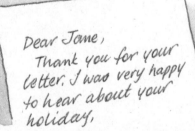

Dear Jane,
Thank you for your letter. I was very happy to hear about your holiday,

**happen**
When something happens, it takes place. What happened to you?

**happy**
Full of joy and very pleased about things.

**hard**
1. Hard is difficult, not easy to do.
2. Hard also means solid and firm. Hard as iron!

**harm**
To do harm is to hurt or damage a person or thing.

**harvest**
To gather in all the crops when they are ready.

**hat**
You wear a hat to cover and protect your head.

**hate**
To hate is to really dislike a thing. I hate washing dishes!

**have**
If you have a thing, you own it. I have long hair now, when I was a baby I had none at all.

**head**
1. The top part of a person's or animal's body.
2. It can also mean the chief or most important thing or person.

**health**
Your health is how your body feels. Healthy is well, unhealthy is ill.

**hear**
You hear sounds through your ears when you listen.

**heart**
Your heart is like a pump that sends the blood round your body.

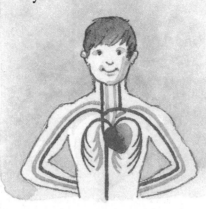

**heat**
Hot things give off heat.

**heavy**
Something heavy weighs a lot.

**heel**
The back of your foot or the back of your shoe is a heel.

**height**
Measure your height from the ground to the top of your head.

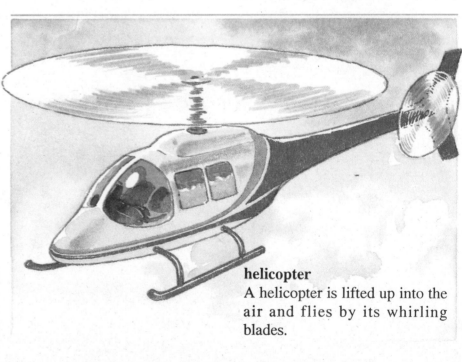

**helicopter**
A helicopter is lifted up into the air and flies by its whirling blades.

**hello**

Hello is a greeting. When you answer the telephone you say hello!

**helmet**

A helmet is a hard hat which protects the head.

**help**

To help is to make things easier for another person. I will help you paint the fence!

**here**

Here is the place you are at this moment. I live here!

**hero**

A hero is a very brave man or boy.

**heroine**

A heroine is a very brave woman or girl.

**hibernate**

When the weather turns cold some animals hibernate and go to sleep for the winter.

**hide**

Will you hide him and keep him out of sight? See that he is well hidden!

**high**

Mountains are very high. They are a long way from the ground.

**hill**

A hill is a small mountain with gently sloping sides.

---

**herbs**

Each herb has a different smell and flavour. These plants are used for medicine and food.

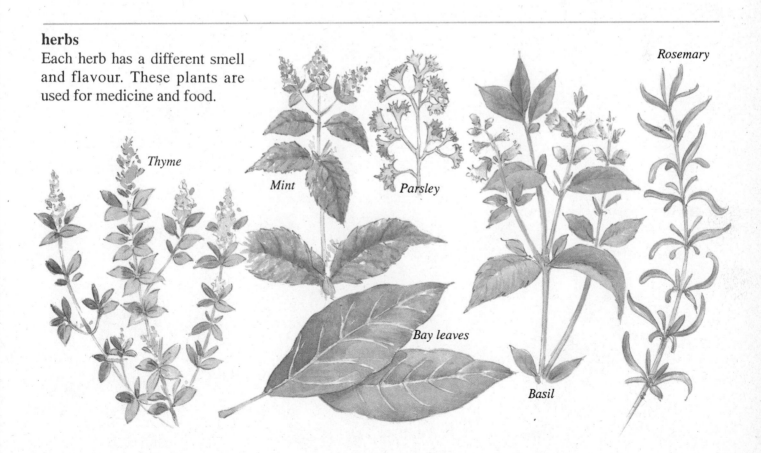

*Rosemary*

*Thyme*

*Mint*

*Parsley*

*Bay leaves*

*Basil*

**his**
His means belonging to a man. Is that jacket really his?

**history**
History is the story of the past. Learning history is often hard!

**hit**
Hit is to strike out or knock something or someone.

**hold**
This tin holds biscuits. Hold out your hand and you can have one!

**hole**
A hole is an opening. It can go right through, or form a hollow.

**hollow**
A hollow has nothing but empty space inside. The conjuror showed us a hollow tube.

**home**
Home is where you live.

**homework**
Work brought from school to be done at home.

**honest**
To be honest is to be truthful.

**hook**
A bent piece of metal for catching hold of things.

**hop**
To bob up and down on one foot. Who is this hopping along?

**hope**
I hope my wish will come true! You really want your wish to happen.

**horizon**
The horizon is the place where the ground and the sky seem to meet.

**horn**
1. The hard part that sticks out of an animal's head.
2. Have you a horn on your bicycle?

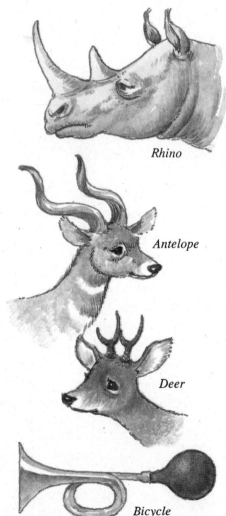

*Rhino*

*Antelope*

*Deer*

*Bicycle*

**hospital**
If you have had an accident or you are ill you go to hospital to be taken care of.

**hot**
Do not touch hot things. They give off heat and could burn you.

**hotel**
When you are away from home, you can pay for a room and a meal in a hotel.

**hour**
Sixty minutes in one hour, twenty-four hours in a day.

**hovercraft**
A hovercraft carries passengers just above the sea or land on a cushion of air.

**how**
This is an asking word; how was that done?

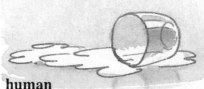

**human**
People, because they think and speak, are human. Animals are not.

**hungry**
I am hungry. I need some food because I lost my lunch!

**hurry**
Hurry up, or we will miss the bus!

**hurt**
Someone who is hurt is in pain. I bet that hurts!

**hutch**
Home for a pet rabbit.

**hurricane**
A violent storm with strong winds that can cause a lot of damage.

# I i

## ice
Ice is frozen water. It is solid, cold and hard.

## iceberg
An iceberg is a mountain of ice floating in the sea.

## ice-cream
Ice-cream is cream and sugar frozen. If you lick it, it melts in your mouth.

## icicle
A spike of ice hanging down where water has dripped and frozen into a point.

## idea
When Sally has a clever idea, she has a clever thought in her mind.

## ill
My brother feels unwell today. I'm sure he is ill.

## immediately
"Take that make-up off immediately!" She means at once.

## impossible
It is impossible to count all the grains of sand. It can't be done.

## indoors
Table tennis is an indoor game, it is played inside.

## infant
A very young child is an infant. It can be a boy or a girl.

## injure
The skier hit a pine tree and was injured. He was hurt badly.

## ink
Your pen is full of a coloured liquid called ink.

## insect
There are many different kinds of insects, all have six legs.

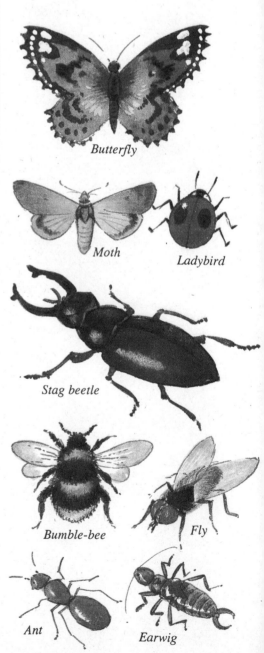

*Butterfly*

*Moth*

*Ladybird*

*Stag beetle*

*Bumble-bee*

*Fly*

*Ant*

*Earwig*

**inside**
You can be inside a room and inside the cupboard. You are not outside, you are within.

**instant**
Quick as a flash! In an instant, the wizard turned the frog into a prince.

**instrument**
Music is played on an instrument. Here are some of them.

Keyboard

Drum

Guitar

Trumpet

Recorder

Triangle

Violin

Tambourine

**introduce**
Baby Bear introduced the girl to his parents. "This is Goldilocks!" he said.

**inventor**
An inventor thinks of something useful that no one has ever thought of before.

**invisible**
Something invisible cannot be seen.

**invite**
To invite is to ask someone to do something. Here is an invitation to my party.

**iron**
1. A hard metal that is used to make steel.
2. I will iron your jeans with my new iron!

**island**
An island is land surrounded by water. Fiji is a small island, Australia is a huge one.

Fiji

Australia

# J j

### jacket
A jacket is a short coat. It can also mean a cover or an outer casing.

### jail
When you are sent to prison you are put in jail.

### jam
1. Jam is made by boiling sugar and fruit together.

2. When things are squeezed tightly together they are jammed. These cars are in a traffic jam.

### jar
A jar is a container with a wide opening at the top. Jars often hold food.

### jaw
Your jaw is the base of your mouth to which your teeth are fixed.

### jealous
I am jealous because she won the cup. I want that cup, although it belongs to her!

### jeans
Trousers made from a thick, cotton cloth called denim.

### jelly
Jelly is made from fruit juice and gelatine. When set, it is clear and wobbly.

### jellyfish
A jellyfish drifts in the sea. Its body is like a jelly and it can sting you!

### jet
A jet is a very fast aircraft driven by a jet engine, not propellers. The engine makes hot gases which escape backwards and thrust the plane forwards.

### jewel
A jewel is a precious stone.

### jewellery
An ornament made of gold and silver and jewels.

**jigsaw**
A picture cut up into pieces for you to fit together again.

**job**
This man is a milkman. It is his job to deliver the milk.

**jog**
When horses jog they trot slowly. People jog to keep fit.

**join**
1. When you join two things, you fasten them together.

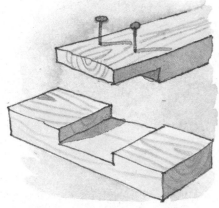

2. When you join a club you become a member. Join the Brownies!

**joke**
A joke is a short story that makes you laugh. Have you heard this joke?

**jolly**
When we hear lots of jokes we feel jolly.

**journey**
When you go on a journey you travel to a place. It can be a short or long trip.

**joy**
When you jump for joy, you are delighted.

**judge**
A person who decides what is right and what is wrong in a dispute.

**jug**
A jug holds liquids and is very easy to pour.

**juggler**
Jugglers entertain you by balancing objects and keeping them in the air at the same time.

**juice**
The liquid squeezed from fruit and vegetables.

**jump**
Spring into the air with both feet off the ground.

**jungle**
A jungle is a tropical forest, it is dense and overgrown.

**juggernaut**
A huge lorry.

# K k

**keen**
If you are keen, you are very willing to do things.

**keep**
To keep is to hold onto something. A miser keeps all his money to himself.

**ketchup**
A thick, tasty sauce you put on food.

**kettle**
You boil water in a kettle. It has a spout for pouring out the water.

**key**
A key fits into a keyhole. You must turn it to unlock the door.

**kick**
When you kick you strike out with your foot. Kick the ball, not your brother!

**kill**
Kill is to make something or someone die. Who killed Cock Robin?

**kilogramme**
The weight of something is measured in kilogrammes.

**kind**
1. Kind means caring towards others.
2. What kind of fruit would you like? This means what sort.

**king**
A king rules his country or kingdom.

**kitchen**
You prepare and cook food in the kitchen. You wash-up too!

**kite**
A kite is made up of paper or cloth on a wooden frame. It flies high in the sky lifted by the wind.

**kitten**
A young cat. Kittens always love to play.

**knee**
This is the joint that makes your leg bend, especially when you kneel.

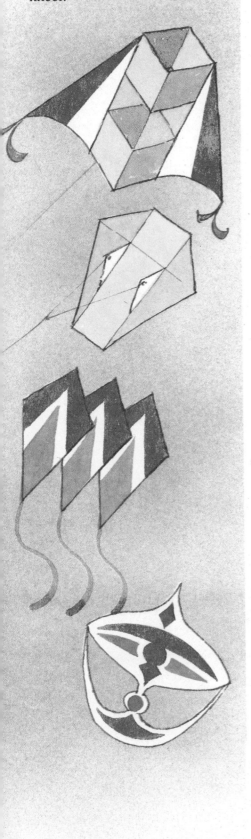

**knight**
Long ago knights wore armour and fought on horseback.

**knit**
When you knit you make a garment by weaving loops of wool together on needles.

**knob**
A round lump on the end or surface of something. When you open a door you turn the knob.

**knock**
Knock at the door, but not too hard, or you will knock it down!

**knot**
When you tie a knot you join two pieces of string together.

*Reef knot*

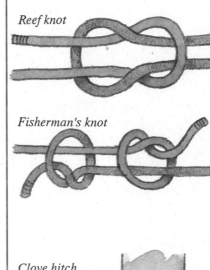

*Fisherman's knot*

*Clove hitch*

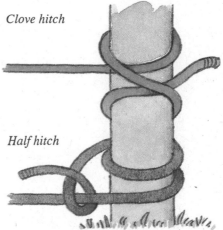

*Half hitch*

*Sheet bend*

**know**
Do you understand how to tie knots? Do you know how to do them? I knew you did!

# L l

**label**
A label tells you about a thing or what is inside.

**ladder**
You climb up the rungs of a ladder to reach high places. Window cleaners always carry their ladders around.

**lake**
A large stretch of water with land all around.

**lamp**
There are many different kinds of lamps and they all give us light.

**land**
1. Land is the surface of the Earth that is not sea.
2. Concorde is about to land at the airport.

**lane**
A narrow road in the country. A narrow street in the town.

**language**
Words used by people to write and speak. There are many different languages.

**large**
Large is big; not little.

**lasso**
A cowboy uses a lasso for roping cattle. It is a long rope with a sliding loop.

**last**
1. Last means after all the others.
2. How long will this noise last? How long will it go on?

**late**
If you are late for school you arrive later than you should.

**laugh**
When people see something funny they laugh. Ha! Ha!

**launch**
When you launch a rocket into space or a ship into the sea, you start it moving.

**lawn**
An area of grass in a garden. It is cut by a lawnmower to keep it short.

**lay**
1. Birds lay eggs. They produce them.
2. When we lay something down, we put it down carefully.

**lazy**
If you are lazy, you don't want to do any work.

**lead**
1. To lead is to show the way.
2. A dog has a lead. It is a strap that fits onto his collar.

**leaf**
Here are some different leaf shapes. Leaves cover trees and plants.

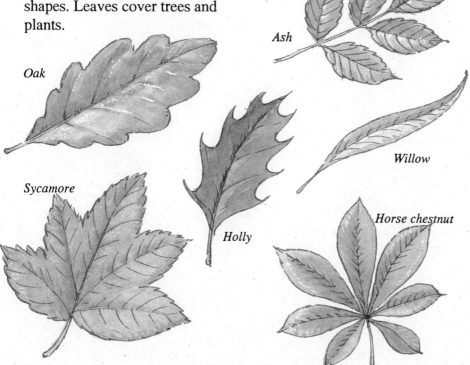

*Oak*

*Ash*

*Willow*

*Sycamore*

*Holly*

*Horse chestnut*

**learn**
You learn if you find out facts or get to know how to do things.

**leave**
When baby birds leave the nest they go away. Leave them alone, they will be back next year!

**left**
Left is opposite to right.

**leg**
Tables, chairs and people are supported by legs.

**legend**
Some say Robin Hood was a legend. Do you believe he was real or just a story?

**lemonade**
A drink made from lemons, water and sugar. It can be very fizzy.

**lend**
To lend is to let a person borrow something for a little while.

**length**
The distance from one end to the other.

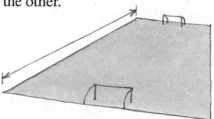

**less**
Less is not as much. I get less pocket money than Jim!

**lesson**
A certain length of time in which you learn.

**letter**
1. You can write a message to someone in a letter.
2. Twenty-six letters make up the alphabet.

**library**
A place where collections of books are kept. Borrow a book from your library!

**lid**
A lid is a cover that closes a container.

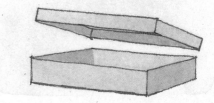

**lie**
1. When you don't tell the truth, you lie.
2. When you lie down, you remain flat.

**life**
Everything alive has life. Life is being alive.

**lifeboat**
A special boat full of brave men who try to save people from drowning in the sea.

**lightning**
It flashes in the sky during a thunderstorm.

**like**
1. If you like a person, you are fond of them.
2. Like can mean almost the same.

**lipstick**
Make-up for your lips. Have I got too much lipstick on?

**liquid**
You can pour a liquid. It flows and is always wet.

**listen**
If you want to hear a sound, you must listen.

**litre**
A litre is used to measure liquids.

**lift**
To raise something up higher. Lift me up!

**light**
1. Things that are not heavy are light.
2. Light comes from the Sun and at night we must use lamps.

**line**
Draw a line! It can be straight or it can be curved.

*1 litre is about 1¾ pints*

**lighthouse**
You will find a lighthouse near dangerous coasts. The winking light on top of the tower warns sailors of danger.

**little**
Little means very small.

**long**
How long is the pencil? How far is it from one end to the other?

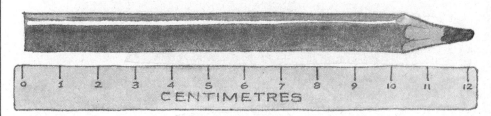

**live**
I live in a house, my fish lives in a bowl. I can't live in the water, he can't live out of it!

**lobster**
A shellfish with a tough shell and two very strong pincers.

**lock**
A lock fastens a door, a chest or a drawer. You must have the right key to unlock it.

**look**
Look up, look down, look all around! You are using your eyes to see.

**loose**
If you have a loose tooth, it is not fixed. It wobbles!

**lorry**
A lorry is a truck that moves goods from place to place by road.

**lose**
When you lose something, although you search, you can't find it.

**lot**
What a lot of lettuce. I've never seen so many!

**loud**
You can hear a loud noise very easily.

**love**
To love someone is to like them as much as you possibly can.

**luggage**
When you go on holiday you take bags and cases full of clothes. Lots of luggage!

**lumberjack**
A man who cuts down trees ready for the mill.

**lunch**
A midday meal. It might be a quick snack or a great big bite!

# Mm

### machine
Machines help us do our work easier and quicker. Here are a few that help us.

*Lawn tractor*

*Hand mixer*

*Vacuum cleaner*

*Garden tiller*

### magic
No one can explain magic. Strange things happen when magic spells are cast!

### magnet
Magnets are made of iron and steel. They attract or pull metal objects towards them.

### magnify
Magnify is to make things bigger. Look under this magnifying glass.

### make
If you make something you put it together. You make the dinner today!

### male
Male is the opposite of female. Men and boys are male.

### man
When a boy grows up he becomes a man.

**many**
Many means a lot. A Dalmatian has many spots.

**map**
A map is a plan of a continent, a country or just a small area.

**march**
To march is to walk in step like soldiers.

**margarine**
This food is made from a blend of vegetable oils. You can spread it on bread or cook with it.

**market**
Lots of things are bought and sold from stalls in the market. Some markets are held out of doors.

**marry**
When a man and woman become husband and wife they marry.

**mask**
A mask covers your face. It can make you look very different.

**match**
1. You can light a match.
2. You can play in a match.
3. You can match things up.

**meadow**
A grass field full of wild flowers and plants.

**meal**
Breakfast, lunch, tea and supper are meals.

**measure**
When we measure something, we find out the size of it or how much there is.

**mechanic**
A person who looks after engines.

**medicine**
If you are ill, medicine will help you get well.

**meet**
I am going to meet my pen friend! We are going to get together.

**melt**
The sun came out and my snowman turned to water. He melted!

**mend**
To mend is to repair something so it will be useful again.

**mermaid**
A legendary sea creature with a woman's body and a fish's tail for legs.

**mess**
If your room is a mess, it is very untidy.

**message**
When you send a message, you send words to another person.

**metal**
Iron, steel, aluminium, copper and tin are all metals.

**method**
A method is a well thought out way to do something.

**metre**
A metre is a measurement of length or height.

**microphone**
It picks up sounds and makes them louder. Pick up the mike!

**microscope**
Tiny objects appear much bigger under a microscope.

**midday**
Midday is twelve noon.

**middle**
The middle is a point in the centre, the same distance from either end.

**midnight**
Twelve o'clock at night, before a new day begins.

**milk**
We drink milk from cows and sometimes goats.

**million**
A thousand thousand.

**miner**
A man who works down a mine.

**minus**
1. Uncle is minus his glasses. He can't see without them.
2. Minus also means to subtract.

$$10 - 6 = 4$$

**minute**
Sixty seconds in a minute. Sixty minutes in one hour.

**mirror**
Look in the mirror! What do you see reflected in the glass?

**miserable**
When my parrot escaped, I felt very miserable.

**miss**
1. I miss my parrot so much. I wish he would come back!
2. I love to play in goal but I often miss the ball!

**mist**
Mist is like a fine rain or a light fog.

**mistake**
To make a mistake is to make an error.

$$2 + 2 = \cancel{5} \; 4$$

**mix**
If you put different things together you mix them.

**money**
We use money when we buy things. We pay in coins and notes.

**monster**
A monster is a huge, horrible, frightening thing.

**month**
There are twelve months in a year.

JANUARY · FEBRUARY · MARCH
APRIL · MAY · JUNE · JULY
AUGUST · SEPTEMBER · OCTOBER
NOVEMBER · DECEMBER

**moon**
The Moon spins round the Earth. The Sun's light catches the Moon and makes it shine.

**moonlight**
When the Moon is full it shines with a silvery light called moonlight.

**more**
Mary has more apples than Ken. She has a greater amount.

**morning**
The morning comes after the night and goes on until midday.

**most**
Sara has the most flowers. She has the greater amount.

**moth**
Moths are not as colourful as butterflies. They fly at night.

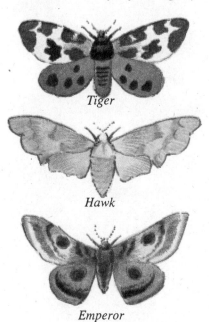

*Tiger*

*Hawk*

*Emperor*

**mother**
A mother is a woman who has had a child or children.

**mountain**
A gigantic hill with steep rocky sides. Some mountain peaks are covered in snow.

**mouth**
You use your mouth to speak and eat. Smile please!

**move**
Nothing stands still, even the Earth is moving all the time.

**mud**
Wet, sticky, soft earth is mud. Wipe your muddy boots!

**mug**
You get more in a mug than a cup. What is your favourite drink in a mug?

**multiply**
You make something several times bigger if you multiply.

6 X 4 = 24

**muscle**
Muscles are parts of the body that produce movement, they can only pull not push. We need two sets of muscles for each joint or limb, one to bend and one to straighten.

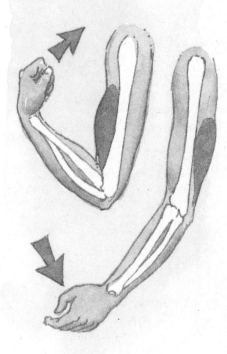

**music**
Different sounds made by instruments or a person's voice are music.

**mystery**
A mystery is something strange or puzzling that you cannot explain.

**motorway**
A modern fast road with three lanes in each direction.

# N n

**nail**

1. A thin piece of metal with a sharp point. You hammer it through two pieces of wood to join them together.

2. Nails are the hard parts on the tips of your fingers and toes.

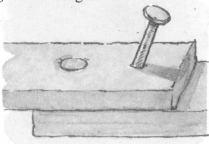

**name**

Each person and every thing has a name. That is what they are called.

**narrow**

This opening is too narrow to squeeze through. It isn't wide enough!

**nasty**

How unpleasant. What a nasty black eye!

**natural**

Made by nature and not by man.

**nature**

The world around us, not changed by man in any way.

**naughty**

To behave badly in a mischievous way.

**navy**

The whole of a country's ships of war and all the sailors.

**nearly**

He nearly fell in the river means he almost did.

**neat**

When you are neat you are tidy and put everything in the proper place.

**need**

When you need a thing it is necessary to have it. This gentleman needs a new suit!

**near**

Near is close. I was so near to the shark I could have touched it!

**needle**
A thin pointed piece of metal with a slit at one end. Poke a thread through the slit and you can begin to sew.

**neighbour**
Someone who lives near by.

**nervous**
I am frightened of the shadows in my room. They make me very nervous.

**net**
A net is for catching things without doing any damage.

**never**
Never is at no time, not ever. You will never be able to lift that!

**new**
Something that has never been worn or has just been made. New is fresh; not old.

**newspaper**
Printed sheets of paper to read. They tell you the news every day.

**next**
You are next in line, so you can sit next to the driver. Next means near.

**nib**
A nib is a pen point.

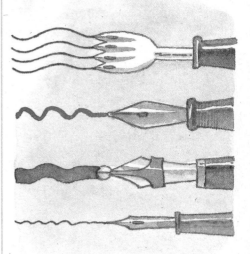

**nibble**
Hamsters nibble their food.

**night**
When the sun has set, it grows dark and night falls.

**nobody**
If a room is empty, there is nobody there!

**noise**
A sound of any kind.

**nest**
Most birds and a few animals make a nest for their young.

*Stork*

*Harvest mouse*

*Coot*

*Woodpecker*

*Swallow*

**none**
Paul had six bricks, Peter had none, not even one.

**noon**
Noon is twelve o'clock midday.

**north**
North is opposite to south. The Arctic Circle and the North Pole are the coldest northern parts of the world.

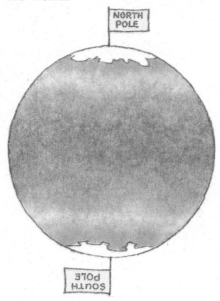

**nose**
You breathe and smell through your nose.

**not**
You are not to throw that! Not is another way of saying no.

**note**
1. Mum wrote Dad a note about his dinner.

2. When you play a tune, you hear and play lots of notes.

**nothing**
Nothing on your plate means not one thing.

**notice**
1. A notice is a written sign for all to read.

2. Have you noticed Tom's arm? Have you seen it?

**nought**
Nought is the name of the figure 0.

**noun**
A noun is the name of anything from apple to zebra.

**now**
I am going for a walk now. Now means at this very moment.

**nowhere**
My hat is nowhere in sight. I can't see it anywhere.

**nuisance**
Something that is annoying. That bonfire is a nuisance.

**number**
A symbol or word that says how many.

**nurse**
A person trained to look after the sick.

**nursery**
A place where little children play and are looked after.

**nut**
A nut has a hard shell with a kernel or seed inside.

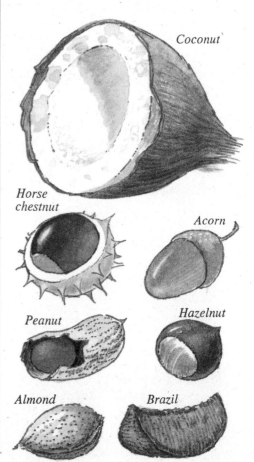

*Coconut*

*Horse chestnut*

*Acorn*

*Peanut*

*Hazelnut*

*Almond*

*Brazil*

# O o

**oak**
The oak is the traditional tree of England. This great tree grows from a tiny acorn.

**oar**
You row a boat with oars.

**oasis**
A fertile place in the desert with water and trees.

**obey**
The Genie of the Lamp obeyed Aladdin. He did as Aladdin told him.

**occupation**
What is this man's occupation? What job does he do?

**ocean**
An ocean is bigger than a sea.

**o'clock**
When we tell the time by the clock we say four o'clock.

**octopus**
A sea creature with eight arms or tentacles.

**odd**
An odd number cannot be divided by two like an even number.

**off**
Switch off the television! Jump off the chair! Off means not on.

**offer**
If you say you will do something, you offer to help. Mother offered Tom a lift.

**office**
People work in an office. It is their place of business.

**officer**
Someone who is in command and gives orders to people in the navy, army, airforce the police or the fire service.

**often**
My dog often digs in the garden. He does it again and again.

**oil**
1. Oil is a greasy, black liquid that is found underground or under the sea bed.
2. We use oil made from seeds and plants for cooking.

*Drilling for oil at sea*

**ointment**
Put some ointment on your knees, they look sore!

**old**
An old person has lived a long time. An old thing has been used a lot and is no longer new.

**only**
James was the only one to win a rosette. No one else did, he was the only one.

**open**
Open means not shut. Alice went through the open door and opened her eyes wide.

**opera**
A musical play with singers instead of actors.

**orchard**
Fruit trees grow in an orchard.

**orchestra**
Many musicians playing together form an orchestra. Their instruments are in four different groups.

**ordinary**
Something ordinary has nothing special about it. What an ordinary house!

**ornament**
Ornaments are a decoration. We get pleasure from seeing them.

**other**
Here are two kittens, one is ginger the other grey. One is different to the other.

**our**
Our ball has been stolen. It belonged to us.

**out**
We are going out to play. The sun is shining outside and we don't want to stay in.

**outline**
Draw an outline of your pet.

**oval**
Anything oval is shaped like an egg.

**oven**
You can roast and bake food in an oven.

**over**
1. The hen flew over the gate.
2. I am sad my holiday is over, or at an end.

**overhead**
The swans flew overhead. They passed above our heads.

**own**
If you own something it belongs to you. I own a puppy called Goldie.

**oxygen**
Oxygen is one of the gases in air that all living things must have to live.

# P p

## pack
Father wants me to pack his shorts, but the case is packed. It is full up.

## paddle
1. Oh dear! My paddle is floating away.
2. I took my baby sister for a paddle in the shallow water.

## page
A page is one side of a piece of paper in a book, magazine or newspaper.

## pain
When you feel a pain it hurts. Your body is telling your brain something is wrong.

## paint
If you paint a picture or a house, you are putting colour on with a brush.

## pair
A pair is two of the same thing. They go together.

## palm
1. Dates and coconuts grow on palm trees. People use their leaves to thatch huts and make mats.

2. Hold out your hand, the inside or front is your palm.

## pancake
Can you toss a pancake? A batter made of eggs, flour and milk is poured into a frying-pan and cooked into a pancake.

## paper
Paper is made from pulped up wood, which is pressed and rolled into sheets.

## parachute
When you jump out of a plane your parachute opens like an umbrella, and you float safely downwards.

## parcel
Something wrapped in paper and fastened with string or tape.

## parents
Mothers and fathers are parents.

## park
1. An open space with grass and trees that everyone can use.
2. Have I parked my car in the wrong place?

**party**
A party is a group of people. When people celebrate they love a party!

**pass**
1. That motorbike is going to pass us.
2. I have lost my bus pass.
3. My auntie has passed her driving test at last.

4. Pass the ketchup please!
5. The cowboy rode through the mountain pass.

**passenger**
A person who travels in a plane, boat, train or motor vehicle.

**passport**
You need your passport to travel from one country to another.

**past**
Something that happened in the past, usually means it happened long ago.

**pastry**
When you rub fat into flour and roll it out with a rolling pin, you have made pastry.

**pat**
If you pat your dog you tap him gently to show you are pleased with him.

**pattern**
1. Do you like to draw or paint a pattern?
2. A dress pattern has shapes that fit together on material. Cut out and sewn together, they make a dress.

**paw**
Animals have paws. Who made these paw marks?

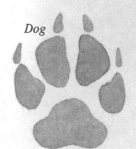

*Dog*  *Fox*  *Badger*  *Cat*  *Mouse*  *Rabbit*

**pay**
When you buy something, you must pay for it with money.

**peace**
Peace means no fighting or war. It can also mean quiet and calm. How peaceful!

**peanut**
Peanuts grow underground. Have you tasted roasted peanuts and peanut butter?

**pearl**
If you are lucky you may find a pearl in an oyster. You need lots of pearls to make a necklace.

**pebble**
Little smooth stones found on beaches or river-beds.

**pedal**
When you pedal your bicycle with your feet on the pedals, you make the wheels move.

**peel**
The peel is the skin of fruit and vegetables. This apple has been peeled.

**pen**
You use a pen for writing with ink.

**pencil**
A pencil is a wooden stick with a thin lead through the middle.

**penknife**
A knife small enough to keep in your pocket. It has blades that fit into the handle.

**people**
Men, women and children are all people.

**perfect**
When a thing is perfect, it has no faults at all. Your sewing is perfect!

**perform**
If you perform something, you carry it out or do it. What a performance!

**perfume**
A sweet smelling scent from flowers or in a bottle.

**person**
Every single man, woman and child is a person. Animals are not.

**pet**
An animal kept at home in your house or garden.

**photograph**
A picture taken with a camera. Do you like having your photo taken?

**piano**
When you play the piano and your fingers press the keys, lots of tiny hammers hit wires and make the different notes.

**pick**
1. If you pick flowers you collect or gather them up.
2. Pick a card! You can choose any one.

**picnic**
A packed meal eaten out of doors.

**picture**
A picture is a drawing or a painting. It can also be a photograph.

**pie**
Something good to eat inside a pastry crust.

**piece**
If you take a piece of pie, you take part of it.

**pile**
Things heaped up on top of each other are in a pile.

**pill**
A pill is medicine made into a little ball or easy-to-swallow shape.

**pillar**
Posts that hold up porches, arches and buildings.

**pillow**
A soft cushion on a bed.

**pilot**
A pilot steers an aeroplane.

**pin**
Shaped like a small needle with a tiny, round head at one end.

**pipe**
1. Does your grandad smoke a pipe?

2. Pipes can carry liquid or gas. They are hollow tubes.

**place**
This is my place at the table! It is your special spot where you are.

**plait**
Strands of hair or lengths of material woven into a pattern.

**plan**
1. A plan is a drawing of an object or a building from above.
2. Those naughty boys have a plan. Have you any idea what it is?

**planet**
There are nine major planets that spin round the Sun. The Earth is one.

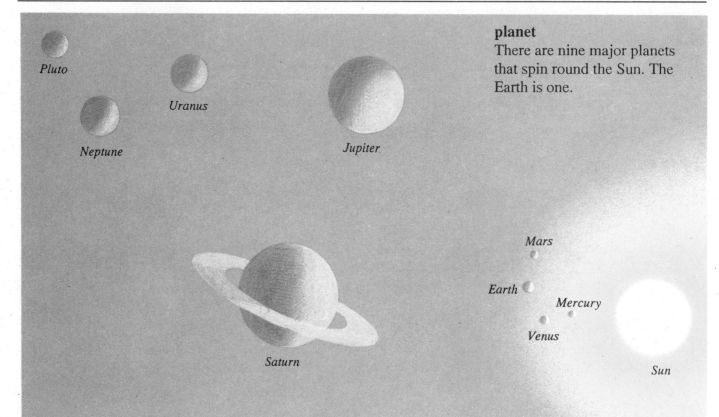

Pluto

Uranus

Neptune

Jupiter

Saturn

Mars

Earth

Mercury

Venus

Sun

**plant**
A plant is a living thing which usually grows in soil. It also needs water, air and sunlight.

**plastic**
A man-made material which can be pressed and moulded into many shapes.

**platform**
1. A raised floor like a small stage.
2. I sat on the platform waiting for the train.

**play**
1. A play is a story which is acted.

2. When you play, forget work and have fun!

**playground**
A place for children to enjoy themselves.

**please**
1. Ask politely, say "please", then you can have a chocolate!
2. My aunt is very pleased with me. I have made her happy.

**plough**
A tractor or horse pulls a plough as it cuts and turns the soil.

**plus**
Two plus two equals four. Plus means to add to.

**poem**
A poem describes something, usually in rhyme. Can you write poetry?

**point**
1. The sharp end of a thing.
2. It's very rude to point.

**police**
People who are trained to keep law and order.

**polite**
If you have good manners and behave well, people will say you are polite.

**pollute**
To make the Earth dirty and dangerous by getting rid of waste carelessly.

**pond**
A pool of water full of interesting wildlife in the water or around its edge.

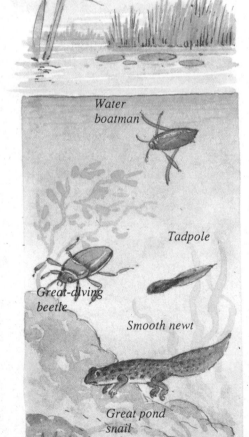

*Water boatman*

*Great-diving beetle*

*Tadpole*

*Smooth newt*

*Great pond snail*

**poor**
If you are poor you have very little money or possessions.

**population**
The number of people that live in one particular place.

**porridge**
Do you eat porridge for your breakfast?

**possible**
If a thing is possible, it can be done.

**poster**
Someone has stuck posters all over this wall.

**postman**
A person who collects and delivers letters and parcels.

**pour**
You pour liquid out of one container into something else.

**powder**
Powder is like dust, very fine and light.

**powerful**
Powerful means very strong. That engine looks really powerful.

**praise**
When you praise a person, you tell them they have done well. Congratulations!

**prepare**
The chef prepared the pizza. He got it ready.

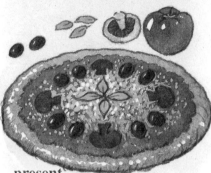

**present**
A present is a gift to give or to receive.

**pretend**
When you pretend, you make-believe. Lucy is pretending she is grown-up.

**pretty**
Doesn't this little girl look pretty. She thinks she does too!

**price**
What price is that melon? How much money do I need to buy it?

**prince**
The son of a king or queen.

**princess**
The daughter of a king or queen.

**print**
A print is an impression or mark, like a fingerprint or footprint.

## printing

Printing words and pictures in a book or newspaper is done on a printing machine. Letters covered in ink are pressed or printed onto paper.

## prize

A reward for winning. This little pig has won first prize.

## problems

Problems are always difficult to solve.

## programme

1. What is your favourite programme on television?
2. Paul collects football match programmes, Sophie saves them from the theatre.

## promise

To give your word and keep it. Dad promised we could go to the zoo.

## protect

All animals and birds protect their young. They shield them from danger and harm.

## proud

Mother was very proud on sports day when Dad won the parents' race.

## prove

To prove is to show something can be done or that it is true.

## pudding

A pudding is the sweet tasting part of a meal.

## puddle

A small pool of water outside in the road or inside on the floor.

## pull

The tug-of-war team pulled hard on the rope. Each side is trying to make the rope come towards them.

## pump

When your tyres are flat, you use a pump to force air into them.

## punch

To punch is to hit hard with your fists. Boxers punch with their gloves on.

## pupil

Here are some pupils from Dinglewood School learning their lessons!

## puppet

Puppets are dolls that move if somebody else pulls the strings.

## purse

A purse is a small bag to keep your money safe.

## push

When you push, you press against something until it moves.

## puzzle

A puzzle is difficult to solve or understand.

## pyjamas

I see you are wearing your pyjamas. You must be ready for bed!

# Q q

**quack**
When ducks make a noise they quack.

**quarrel**
If you quarrel with someone, you get angry and argue.

**quarter**
Cut a thing into four equal parts and you have four quarters. One of the parts is a quarter.

**queen**
A woman who rules a country or the wife of a king.

**question**
You ask a question to find out something. What is on the blackboard? The answer to that question is, a question mark!

**quick**
Quick means fast or speedy. Be quick! Then you will win the rally.

**quiet**
To be quiet is to be silent and make no noise at all.

**quilt**
A padded cover for a bed. Here is a patchwork quilt.

**quiz**
A quiz is like a test. You must answer a number of questions.

**queue**
A line of people or vehicles waiting their turn.

# R r

### radar
Radar is a way of finding out how far away objects are, by using radio waves.

### raft
A raft is a floating platform, sometimes made of logs lashed together.

### rain
When it rains, water drops from clouds in the sky and falls down to Earth.

### rainbow
Rainbows are caused by sunlight shining through raindrops. A rainbow is split up into seven colours.

### rare
Something rare is uncommon. There are not many of them.

### raw
Raw meat and vegetables are not cooked.

### ray
Rays from a lamp are beams of light. Sunbeams are thin rays of sunlight.

### razor
Father shaves with a razor. It has a very sharp blade.

### reach
1. To reach is to stretch towards something.
2. We have reached the sea at last. We have got there.

### read
You look at words and understand them.

### ready
Are you ready to go camping? Are you prepared with all you need?

### real
This is not a real man, it's a toy. The little boy is just pretending he's real.

### receive
To receive something is to be given it.

### recipe
A recipe tells you how to make a dish and what to put in it.

Strawberry Mousse
1lb Strawberries
3 Eggs
4oz Sugar
10oz Cream
1tsp Gelatine

## recite

When you recite a poem, you say it out loud.

## record

1. Put a record on the record-player and dance to the music.
2. This pole-vaulter has just set a new world record.

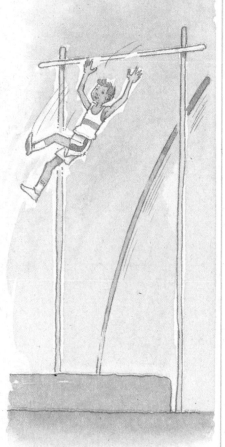

## referee

A referee makes sure the players keep to the rules of the game.

## refrigerator

An ice-cold cupboard that keeps food fresh and cool.

## remain

Father remained to fix the leak. He stayed behind and we left!

## remember

To keep something in your mind and not forget. Remember the steep hill!

## remind

When you remind someone you jog their memory. Did you remember to water my plant?

## remove

Remove your muddy shoes. Take them off!

## repair

Broken things must be repaired.

## reply

To reply is to answer. "Who are you?" asked Alice. "The White Rabbit," he replied.

## reporter

A reporter interviewed us today. Perhaps we shall be on television or in the newspapers tomorrow.

## reptile

A cold blooded creature with a scaly skin.

*Tortoise*

*Crocodile*

*Snake*

*Lizard*

**rescue**
If you save a person from danger you rescue them.

**rest**
1. When you feel tired, sit down and rest.
2. Leave the washing-up. I will do the rest of it later.

**restaurant**
Meals are served in a restaurant. You get a bill when you have finished.

**return**
1. When John returned my model, it was broken.
2. Swallows come to Britain in March and return to Africa in September.

**reward**
A reward is like a prize. Sometimes you are given a reward for finding something.

**rhyme**
1. Words that sound the same.
2. Rhymes are small poems like nursery rhymes.

**rhythm**
Shake a tambourine in time to the music and you've got rhythm.

**rice**
Rice is a grain like grass. It grows in fields flooded with water.

**ride**
To be carried along by a machine or an animal.

**right**
1. Right is opposite to left.
2. Am I right in thinking you come from Australia?

**ring**
1. A ring fits your finger.
2. A ring can be a circle shape.
3. Bells ring ding-a-dong!

**rink**
A very large area with plenty of room for ice-skating or roller skating.

**ripe**
When fruit is ripe, it is ready to eat.

**rise**
Get up in the morning, rise and shine. The sun has risen in the sky.

**river**
Rivers begin in the hills as small streams. They grow deeper and wider then flow into the sea.

**road**

A road is a way on which people and vehicles travel.

**roar**

When lions and tigers make a noise, they roar.

**rob**

To rob is to steal. There's been a robbery at the bank, and the robber is getting away!

**robe**

Here is the mayor in his robes. Doesn't he look grand.

**robot**

A mechanical man. Andrew has a toy robot.

**rock**

1. Rock the baby's cradle from side to side.
2. A rock is a large stone. Rock climbing can be dangerous.

**rocket**

1. A firework on a stick.
2. Astronauts travel through space in a rocket.

**roll**

The wheel went rolling down the hill, it turned over and over.

**roof**

The roof covers the top of a building.

**room**

Rooms are different parts of a building or house.

**root**

Dig up a plant, growing beneath the soil are the roots.

**rope**

A long thick twisted cord made up of lots of thin cords.

**rough**

1. The sea looks rough today.
2. What a rough hand you have, Mr. Gorilla.

**round**

A circle has a round shape and so has a ball.

**row**

1. These flowers are planted in a row.

2. Row your boat on the lake.

**rub**

To move and press one thing hard against another. Rub your shoes.

**rubber**

1. Rubber comes from the sap of a tree. Lots of things we use every day are made from it.
2. Jenny made a mistake in her drawing and rubbed it out with her rubber.

**rubbish**

Throw out all that rubbish! You don't need it any more.

**rule**

Rules are orders that must be obeyed.

**ruler**

1. A ruler is a person that governs a country.
2. We use a ruler to measure things.

**run**

Here are some runners running a race. How fast can you run?

**rung**

Climb up the ladder rung by rung.

# S s

**sad**
Sally is sad, she is feeling very unhappy about something.

**saddle**
A seat on a bicycle or a horse.

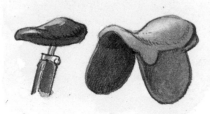

**safe**
Now he is safe, he is not in any danger.

**sail**
When the wind fills the sails the boat sails along. These sailors have sailed many a sea.

**salad**
Vegetables or fruit eaten without cooking.

**same**
These twins look the same. They are alike except for the smudge on Gary's nose.

**sand**
Grains of sand are made by rocks and shells ground down by the weather and sea.

**sandal**
An open shoe with straps.

**sandwich**
To make a sandwich you put your favourite food between two slices of bread.

**sauce**
Sauces add flavour to food.

**save**
1. When you save money you keep it to use later.
2. If you are a lifeguard you are trained to save lives.

**scales**
1. A weighing machine.
2. The hard flakes on the skin of fish and snakes.
3. Musical exercises.

**school**
Pupils go to school to learn. At the beginning they are taught to read and write.

**science**
In science we learn things by experiments, study and careful testing.

**scissors**
Scissors have two sharp blades fixed in the middle. They can cut paper, cloth and even your hair.

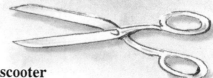

**scooter**
This is my brother's scooter. Here I am on mine!

**scream**
My mouse escaped and made my sister scream.

**screw**
A screw is like a nail with grooves, which fastens wood together. You use a screwdriver to turn a screw.

**sculptor**
A sculptor carves objects in stone and wood. They are called sculptures.

**sea**
Sea is salt water that covers a great part of our Earth.

**search**
When I searched for my tie, I looked everywhere.

**season**
There are four seasons, each one is a quarter of a year.

**seaweed**
Plants that grow in the sea.

**secret**
Something only one person knows, until they tell somebody else.

**see**
I can see you! Can you see me?

**seed**
New plants grow from the seeds of the old plants.

**sell**
The greengrocer sells fruit. He sold me a pineapple.

**see-saw**
One side goes up, as the other side goes down.

**self**
When I'm by myself, I'm all alone. Myself is me.

**send**
Send Tim to fetch the coal. Make him go and get it.

**sentence**
I broke my leg and had to walk on crutches. That sentence tells you in a few words a complete happening.

**sentry**
A soldier on guard. This soldier has a sentry box.

**several**
Several is more than one, perhaps two or three. Sue has several swimsuits.

**sew**
A needle and thread and a piece of cloth is all you need to sew.

**shadow**
When the sun is shining, your shadow goes everywhere with you.

**shake**
To shake something you move it up and down or from side to side.

**shallow**
Shallow water is not deep.

**shampoo**
I get shampoo in my eyes every time Dad washes my hair!

**shape**
Everything and everybody has a different shape.

**share**
When I shared my grapes with Kim, I gave her part of them.

**sharp**
Don't play with knives. They are sharp and can cut you.

**shed**
A little hut for storing tools and all kinds of things.

**sheet**
1. Mother has the sheets from the beds hanging on the line.
2. Writing letters can use sheets and sheets of paper.

**shelf**
The shelf in my room was full up, so my Dad put up two more shelves.

**shell**
Eggs and nuts have a hard shell covering. So do some animals and sea creatures to protect themselves.

**shelter**
Shelter under my umbrella, it will protect you from the rain!

**shine**
1. If the sun shines it gives out a bright light.
2. When I have polished my shoes, they really shine.

**shop**
Different shops sell different things. What will you buy today?

**short**
Short is neither tall nor long. Which is the shortest pencil?

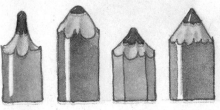

**shorts**
Doing sports we all wear shorts!

**shout**
People shout when they want to be heard.

**shower**
1. A shower is a sprinkling of rain.
2. Taking a shower on a hot day is very refreshing.

**shrink**
If you have a shower in your suit, it will shrink.

**shut**
When a thing is shut, it is closed; not open.

**sick**
I don't feel well today. I feel sick.

**sign**
A sign is a notice that tells you something.

**ship**
A large boat which can cross oceans.

**silent**
To be silent is to keep quiet.

**silk**
A fine thread spun by silkworms and woven into cloth.

**silver**
A precious metal that shines when polished.

**similar**
This book is similar to the other. It is almost the same.

**simple**
This game is simple, not difficult at all.

**sing**
You make music with your voice when you sing a song.

**sink**
1. The kitchen sink is full of dishes.

2. If your boat has a hole, it will sink.

**size**
How big or how small you are is your size.

**skeleton**
All the bones in your body fit together and form your skeleton.

**ski**
Here is a skier skiing down a ski slope.

**skin**
Humans and animals have skin covering their body. Fruit and vegetables have skin too.

**sky**
The sky is up above you. It can be blue in the day, black at night, and sometimes grey and cloudy.

**skyscraper**
Skyscrapers are such high buildings, they seem to touch the sky.

**sleep**
Animals, birds and people, go to sleep to rest.

**slice**
To slice is to cut into flat thin pieces.

**slow**
Slugs and snails can't speed along, they always go slow!

**small**
Small is little; not big or tall.

**smell**
Some things smell lovely, some things smell terrible. Your nose will tell you.

**smile**
You smile and look happy when you are pleased.

**smoke**
As a fire burns it gives off smoke.

**smooth**
A smooth thing has no bumps or sharp bits.

**sneeze**
When something tickles our nose, like pollen or dust, we sneeze.

**snow**
Tiny crystals of ice which form snowflakes then fall from the sky as snow.

**soap**
A good wash with soap and water makes the dirt disappear.

**soft**
Fur and feathers are soft to the touch, not hard at all.

**soil**
Plant a seed in the soil and watch it grow.

## soldier

A soldier is a man in the army. These are soldiers from the past.

*British 1815*

*American 1812*

*German 1812*

*British 1814*

*Belgian 1789*

## solve

To solve a puzzle or a mystery is to find the answer.

## something

You never say what "something" actually is. I have something to show you!

## sometime

Sometime is no real time, just every so often. I will fix the roof sometime!

## son

A son is the boy child of a mother and father.

## song

A song is like a poem or rhyme set to music.

## soon

I will go to bed soon, in a little while.

## sorry

1. I felt sorry that the blackbird died. It made me feel sad.

2. Sorry I broke your vase. I do apologise.

## sound

Every noise you hear is a sound.

## soup

Soup is a liquid food with lots of flavour, made from meat and vegetables.

## sour

Some fruits like gooseberries and rhubarb taste sour.

## south

South is the point opposite to north. Countries with the word south in their name are usually hot.

## space

A space is a place with nothing in it. There is no picture below, just a space.

## speak

When you speak on the telephone you say something to the person at the other end.

## special

Something special is not ordinary but different. Christmas is a special time.

## speed

Speed is the rate you travel. High speed or low speed.

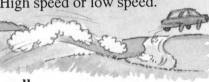

## spell

1. Witches love casting evil spells.

2. To put the letters of a word in the right order.

## spend

1. How much money will I have to spend to buy that?
2. I spend a lot of time at my Grandmother's house.

## spill

When you knock over some liquid you spill it.

## spin

1. A top spins when it turns round and round.
2. You make a thread when you spin on a spinning wheel.
3. A spider spins to make a web.

## splash

Jump into a pool. You will hear the splash as the water splashes out.

**sport**
Sport is a game or pastime.

Golf

American football

Soccer

Netball

Tennis

Cricket

Baseball

**spot**
A spot is a little mark. Spots are lots of little marks.

**spread**
When the baker spreads icing on a cake, he covers the top evenly.

**spring**
The first season of the year. Winter has passed and things start to grow.

**square**
A square has four corners and four straight sides of the same length.

**squeeze**
When you squeeze a lemon, you crush it or press it hard.

**stable**
A building where horses are kept.

**stairs**
Steps for walking up and down to different levels of a building.

**stamp**
1. Stick a stamp on an envelope, then a rubber stamp will stamp the letter.

2. Do you stamp your foot in temper?

**stand**
Stand up, get on your feet! Don't sit there all day!

**star**
You can see stars at night as twinkling points of light in the dark sky. They are objects in space millions of kilometres away.

**start**
To start a thing is to begin it.
Start the race!

**station**
Travellers on trains and buses
arrive and depart at the station.

**stationary**
When a vehicle or person has
stopped and is no longer moving.

**stationery**
Writing paper, pens, pencils,
erasers are all stationery, sold at
the stationers.

**stay**
Stay where you are. Don't move
from that spot!

**steal**
To steal is to take things that
don't belong to you. The
magpie stole the necklace!

**steam**
When water boils it turns into a
misty cloud called steam.

**steep**
A hillside that is steep, slopes
sharply up and down.

**step**
Walk forward, back, and to the
side, you are taking steps.

**stick**
1. Chop the logs into sticks.
2. Stick the paper on the wall.

**sting**
Bees and wasps have a sting in
their tails.

**stir**
If you stir something with a
spoon, you mix it up and move
it round.

**stitch**
Push a needle and thread in and
out of cloth and you have
stitches.

**stop**
To stop is to cease what you are
doing.

**store**
Animals store food for the
winter. It is kept in a safe place
until it is needed.

**storm**
Thunder, lightning, wind and
rain all add up to a storm.

**story**
Tell me a story about Aladdin.
Is it true or made up?

**straight**
Draw a straight line with a ruler.

**stranger**
A stranger is someone you don't
know. Don't talk to strangers!

**stream**
A little river of fresh running
water.

**street**
A road with houses and shops
on both sides.

**stretch**
If you stretch a thing it gets
longer or wider. When you
stretch you reach out.

**stretcher**
He was carried off to hospital
on a stretcher.

**stripe**
Stripes are lines of different
colours.

**strong**
Strong is powerful. Look at this
strong man lifting weights.

**submarine**
A boat that can sail on top of the water, then dive underneath and stay there.

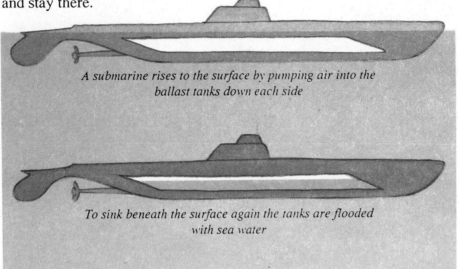

*A submarine rises to the surface by pumping air into the ballast tanks down each side*

*To sink beneath the surface again the tanks are flooded with sea water*

**subtract**
Subtract is to take away.

$$12 - 5 = 7$$

**sudden**
All of a sudden an owl flew out of the tree. It happened unexpectedly.

**sugar**
Sugar makes things sweet. It comes from sugar cane and sugar beet.

**suit**
Is that your new suit? The trousers are too short and the jacket is too long!

**sum**
When you add two or more numbers together, the total is the sum.

**summer**
The warmest season of the year. We hope it is hot on our summer holidays.

**sun**
The Sun gives us light and heat although it is about 93 million miles away from Earth.

**sunburn**
If we stay too long in the hot sun we go red and get painful sunburn.

**supermarket**
A huge store full of all kinds of food and other goods to buy.

**supper**
A snack to have at bedtime.

**sure**
I am sure my invitation said come in fancy dress. I am quite certain!

**surf**
Huge waves that crash onto the shore. Dare you ride the surf on a surfboard?

**surgery**
You visit a surgery to see a doctor or dentist.

**surname**
Your surname is your family name.

**surprise**
If you don't expect something to happen, it comes as a surprise.

**sweet**
1. A pudding at the end of a meal.
2. This bag of sweets taste sweet.
3. This little kitten looks so sweet.

**swim**
Everybody ought to learn to swim to be safe in the water.

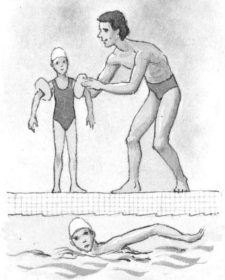

# T t

### table
A piece of furniture with four legs and a flat top.

### tadpole
A tiny, black creature that wriggles out of frog-spawn, grows quickly and becomes a frog.

### tail
A tail is the piece at the end. Animals' tails are at the end of their bodies.

### take
When you take something you hold it with your hands. Sometimes you take things from one place to another, like taking the dog for a walk.

### tall
Tall is high. A giraffe is tall but the trees are taller.

### tame
Some animals are friendly and happy with people. They are tame not wild.

### tap
1. To knock gently is to tap.
2. Turn off the tap as quick as you can!

### tape recorder
A machine that can record sound on tape and play it back.

### taste
We taste with our tongue, bitter, sweet or sour. When you eat a thing you taste it.

### teacher
A teacher helps you to understand about many things. My teacher is teaching me all about Egypt.

### team
A team is a group of people or animals working or playing together.

### telephone
You can speak to someone far away on a telephone. Your voice is carried along wires to another phone.

*Telephone exchange*

### telescope
When you look through a telescope you can see a long way, the lens makes things look bigger and nearer.

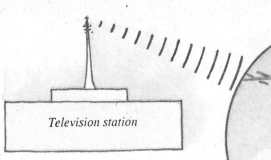

Television station

**television**
A television gives us pictures and sounds from signals sent through the air a long distance away. We need an aerial to receive them.

**tell**
"I must tell you what happened to me." Then Joe told us all about his accident.

**temperature**
How hot or cold something is. The instrument that measures temperature is a thermometer.

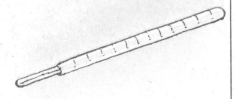

**tent**
A canvas shelter that you can fold up and take anywhere.

**terrible**
Last night there was a terrible fire. It was dreadful and very frightening.

**test**
1. We are having a maths. test to find out how much we know.
2. The man tested the hose and found it was working.

**thank**
If you are grateful for something, you say thank you.

**theatre**
You go to see a play or show in a theatre.

**there**
"There" is somewhere else, it is not here. The balloon is over there. There it goes towards the mountain!

**thick**
Wear a thick coat as the snow is very thick on the ground.

**thin**
Thin is opposite to thick. The oak tree trunk is thick, the silver birch is thin.

**think**
When you think, you are using your brains. Think about this problem.

**thirsty**
To be thirsty is to want a drink. Little children always feel thirsty in the middle of the night!

**thousand**
Ten hundreds are one thousand.

**through**
Through means from one side to the other. The builder knocked a hole through our wall!

**throw**
When you throw something you make it move through the air away from you.

**ticket**
A ticket shows how much you paid for something or to go somewhere.

**tie**
1. A tie is fastened round the neck in a knot or bow.
2. To tie a thing is to fasten it securely.

**tight**
This man's shirt is too tight. His buttons are popping off. It fits him too closely.

**timber**
Timber is wood which has been cut into pieces ready to use in building.

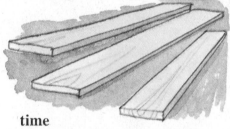

**time**
Time measures how long things take. What time did you leave school? Is it time to go yet?

**tired**
I'm so tired, I need a rest!

**toboggan**
A sledge turned up at the front for sliding down snowy slopes.

**today**
Today is this very day. It's Fred's birthday today!

**together**
Lucy and her cat play together every day. They are with each other all the time.

**tomorrow**
It is Saturday today. Tomorrow it will be Sunday.

**tonight**
1. Tonight is the night after this day.
2. Mum is getting ready to go out tonight.

**tool**
There are lots of different tools that help us do our work.

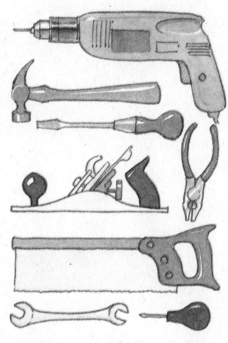

**tooth**
This baby has one tooth, soon he will have many more. You use your teeth to bite and chew. Look after them with a toothbrush and toothpaste.

**top**
The highest point of anything is the top.

**torch**
You can carry a torch in your hand, it gives a narrow beam to light your way in the dark.

**touch**
To touch is to feel with your hand. Wet paint, don't touch!

**tough**
Tough things are hard and don't break easily. My sister's rock cakes are tough!

**towel**
A soft, thick cloth for drying pots and people.

**tower**
A tall, high, narrow building or just part of one.

**town**
A town is full of people, streets, shops and houses. It is not as big as a city.

**tractor**
A tractor pulls farm machinery and moves heavy loads.

**traffic**
All vehicles that move are traffic, along the roads or in the air.

**traffic lights**
These lights control moving traffic at busy junctions and crossroads.

**train**
An engine pulling carriages or wagons along a track.

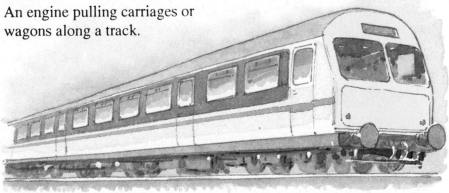

**true**
Something that is true is certain and not a lie. Is it true that chameleons change colour?

**trampoline**
Jump on the trampoline, see how high you can spring!

**transparent**
You can see right through things that are transparent.

**trap**
If an animal is caught in a trap it can't escape. It is trapped.

**trapeze**
Look at the girl swinging high up on the trapeze.

**travel**
To travel is to go from one place to another.

**treasure**
I think they have found buried treasure.

**tree**
A tree lives longer than any other plant. It has a trunk, branches and leaves.

**triangle**
A shape with three sides joined.

**trick**
Can a magician really saw a lady in half, or is it a trick?

**trolley**
Do you ever ride in a supermarket trolley with the shopping?

**trouble**
If you upset a person or make things difficult, you are causing trouble.

**truck**
A truck is an open lorry for carrying goods.

**try**
Try to climb to the top. Do your best and try hard!

**t-shirt**
A vest with short sleeves shaped like a T.

**tunnel**
When a train goes into a tunnel it travels through a long dark passage cut through the ground.

**turn**
If something turns it goes round. Watch me turn a cartwheel!

**typewriter**
This office machine has lots of keys with a letter on each one. When they are pressed they print words on paper.

**tyre**
When the tyres of your bicycle are full of air, they help you ride along smoothly.

**twin**
A twin is one of two children born at the same time to one mother. Animals often have twins too.

# U u

**ugly**
Cinderella's sisters were not pretty, they were Ugly Sisters.

**umbrella**
We open our umbrella to shield us from the rain, then close it when the rain stops.

**uncle**
The brother of your mother or father is your uncle.

**under**
Under means below. What are you doing under the table?

**understand**
If you understand something you know what it means.

**underwear**
The clothes worn next to your skin.

**undress**
To take off your clothes.

**unhappy**
This little girl looks unhappy. I wonder why?

**unicorn**
A fairy tale animal with the body of a horse and a horn on its head.

**uniform**
Uniforms are the clothes of the same kind of people.

*Fireman*          *Nurse*

*Policeman*        *Post lady*

**unkind**
The other birds were unkind to the Ugly Duckling. They were cruel and hurt his feelings.

**untidy**
Do you think this little boy is untidy?

**up**
To go up is to rise. Up is the opposite of down.

**upside-down**
When you are upside-down, you are the wrong way up.

**upstairs**
Jane is climbing the stairs to bed. Her room is upstairs.

**urgent**
These medicines are very urgent. A patient needs them at once!

**useful**
Useful things are helpful. This bucket is useful, just right for the job.

**useless**
Useless things are of no use at all. This bucket is quite useless.

# V v

## vacant
This house is vacant. It is empty with nothing and nobody inside.

## valley
The lower ground that lies between two hills.

## van
A van is a covered truck with sides and a top. Have you ever moved house in a furniture van?

## vanish
When things vanish, they disappear without a trace.

## varnish
A paint which has a glossy finish. My sister is always varnishing her nails!

## vase
You put flowers in a vase. Make sure they have some water.

## vegetable
A plant grown for food that is not a fruit.

Cabbage

Cucumber

Tomato

Turnip

Carrot

Onion

Lettuce

Beans

Potato

Mushroom

Peas

Sweetcorn

## vehicle
Anything that carries goods or people from place to place. Cars, lorries, buses, even wagons and carts are all vehicles.

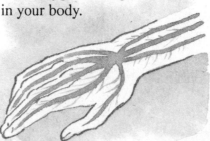

## vein
Blood returns to the heart for more oxygen through the veins in your body.

## verb
Verbs tell of something being done. Swing, jump, laugh, play, are all verbs.

## verse
"There was a bee sat on a wall. It said buzz and that was all!"

## vet
Vet is short for veterinary surgeon. A person who cares for sick animals.

## viaduct
A road or railway bridge over a valley.

## victory
When people or teams compete, one must lose and the other wins the victory.

**video recorder**
A machine that records sounds and pictures on tape, then plays them back through your television.

*The TV signal is picked up by the aerial on the roof. It then goes into the video where it can be recorded. And then onto the TV where you can see the picture.*

**video tape**
A special tape for recording sounds and pictures in a video recorder.

**view**
This artist is painting the view. He is painting the landscape as far as he can see.

**village**
A village is much smaller than a town. It is in the country surrounded by farmland.

**vinegar**
Vinegar tastes sharp like lemon juice. It is used on food and in pickles.

**violin**
A musical instrument with four strings played with a bow.

**visit**
When someone calls to see you they pay you a visit. They are a visitor.

**vitamins**
Vitamins help to make your body strong and healthy. They are found in many foods.

**voice**
You open your mouth and use your voice to speak.

**volcano**
A mountain that throws out red-hot lava, ash and gases through a hole in the top.

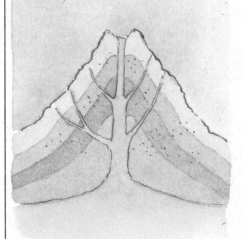

**vowels**
The letters a, e, i, o, u are vowels.

**voyage**
A long journey far across the sea.

# Ww

## wagon
Carts or trucks that can carry heavy loads from place to place by road or rail.

## waist
You wear a belt round your waist. A waistcoat is a jacket without sleeves that just reaches your waist.

## walk
We use our legs and feet to walk. We move along by putting one foot in front of the other.

## wall
A boundary made of bricks or stones, also the side of a house.

## want
This little girl wants her mother. She needs her and wishes she would come.

## warm
Warm is between hot and cold. It's cold outside. Come and warm yourself by the fire!

## warn
If someone is in danger and you tell them about it, you warn them.

## wash
When we are dirty, water washes us clean. Most things come clean with water.

## washing machine
A machine for washing lots of dirty clothes in a short time.

## watch
1. You wear a watch on your wrist to tell you the time.
2. This boy is going to watch the match. He loves looking at football.

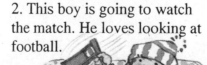

## water
All living things need water to live. Water falls to Earth as rain, filling rivers, lakes and oceans.

## watering can
We need water to drink and so do plants. When it is dry, water the flowers with a watering can.

## wave
1. The Queen waved to me as she went by, and I waved my flag.
2. The surface of the sea moves up and down in waves.

## way
1. How you do something is the way you do it. This is the way to stand on your head!

2. Do you know the way to the Moon?

## wear
You wear clothes on your body. Dad is wearing his gardening clothes. The knees are worn out.

## weather
Everybody talks about the weather. Is it wet or dry today? Will it rain, snow or blow?

**weed**
Gardeners think weeds are a nuisance, they pull them up because they are wild plants.

**week**
A week has seven days. There are fifty-two weeks in a year.

**weigh**
If you weigh something you find out how heavy it is. How much do you weigh?

**wheel**
A wheel is a round shape that turns on its axle or centre. Wheels help things move more easily.

**wheelbarrow**
A little cart with one wheel in front and two handles and legs behind.

**when**
When will the train come? I shall lift your luggage aboard when you get on!

**where**
Where is my tie? It is where you left it.

**which**
Which watch has the second hand? Which asks what thing out of two or more things.

**whisker**
What a fine set of whiskers!

**whisper**
A whisper is a soft little voice. Whisper in my ear!

**who**
Who did that? Who threw that? Who broke that? "Who" asks "Whatever" person.

**whole**
Something that is whole is all there, nothing is missing. Mark said he could eat a whole French loaf!

**why**
"Why are you dressed like that?" When someone asks why, they want to know the reason. "I am going to play American football!"

**wide**
This river is wide, it is broad not narrow.

**wigwam**
American Indians lived in tents called wigwams. They are made from poles covered in animal skins or tree bark.

**wild**

Animals that are wild are not tame. Plants that are wild grow in fields and hedgerows and not in a garden.

**wind**

The wind is air that is moving. Some winds are just a gentle breeze. See what a strong wind can do!

**wind**

To wind is to turn and twist. You wind up the clock by turning the key. Here is a road winding up a steep mountain side.

**windmill**

A mill that is driven by the force of the wind pushing the sails round. Windmills are used for grinding corn or pumping water.

**window**

A window in a building is made of glass to let in light. It can be opened to let in fresh air.

**windscreen**

A transparent shield in a vehicle to stop the wind and rain getting inside. It protects the passengers.

**wing**

All flying things have wings to help them fly. Birds, insects and aeroplanes need wings.

**winter**

The coldest season of the year. Nights are long and dark and the days are short and cold with frost and snow.

**wire**

Wire is a thread made of metal. Different wires carry electricity and telephone messages to our houses.

**wish**

Make a wish! Don't tell me what it is! You really would like that wish to come true.

**witch**

Witches cast magic spells, but only in fairy stories!

**wizard**

A wizard is a man from legends and stories who can work magic. Do you believe he can?

**woman**

When a girl grows up she becomes a woman.

**wood**

1. A small group of trees, not as big as a forest, is called a wood.
2. Wood is a material that comes from trees. It is used in buildings and furniture and many other ways. Things made of wood are wooden.

**wool**

The wool from a sheep's back is spun into yarn then woven into cloth. Woollen clothes are warm and soft.

**work**

When anyone works they do a job. What work does this woman do?

**world**

Everything around us is our world. The Earth and sky is the world in which we live.

**wrap**

When it is cold mothers wrap up their babies before they go out. They cover them up tightly.

**write**

When you write you put down words. You could write a few words, a letter, a story or a whole book.

**wrong**

Something wrong is not right or correct. This is a wrong answer. Sarah has got it wrong.

## x-ray

Have you ever had a broken bone x-rayed? Invisible x-rays from a camera can pass through your flesh and take photographs which show doctors the inside of your body.

## xylophone

A musical instrument made of pieces of wood or metal, each making a different note when hit by a hammer held in either hand.

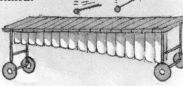

## yacht

A yacht travels fast when the wind fills its sails.

## yard

Yards are areas of hard ground outside houses and schools.

## yawn

When you are tired or bored, you open your mouth wide and yawn.

## year

This baby is one-year-old. She has lived 12 months or 52 weeks or 365 days.

## yesterday

If today is Sunday, yesterday was Saturday.

## yoga

My sister is practising her yoga. She is doing exercises and thinking.

## yoghurt

A food made from milk which tastes thick and creamy. Which flavour do you like?

## yolk

The yellow part of an egg.

## young

When you are young, you are not grown-up. Everyone was young once!

## your

Something that is yours belongs to you. I know this is your note-book. It has your name all over it.

## zebra

A zebra is an African wild horse with stripes.

## zero

Zero is nothing, none, 0.

## zigzag

A line with sharp angles. If you travel in a zigzag you move suddenly from side to side.

## zip

A zip has two sets of metal or plastic teeth that grip each other and fasten things together.

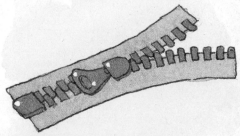

## zoo

A zoo is the place to see all kinds of different animals. Most of the animals are kept in enclosures or cages.